Be advised

How to use consulting effectively

Logica Business Consulting Collection

We've written the Logica Business Consulting Collection with business leaders and managers in mind. You'll find out new practices and technologies that can help you improve your performance and overcome challenges at work.

- Abou-Harb, Georges et Rivard, François,
  L'EAI au service de l'entreprise évolutive

- Delafargue, Bertrand et Rivard, François,
  Repenser le pilotage de l'entreprise

- Hammer, Michael,
  Carnet de route pour manager

- Moore, Geoffrey,
  Sur la ligne de faille

Be advised

How to use consulting effectively

Fiona Czerniawska   François Rivard

LAURENT DU MESNIL●EDITEUR

Fiona Czerniawska is a leading commentator on the consulting industry. She is the joint founder and managing director of Source (www.sourceforconsulting.com) which aims to help clients purchase consulting services in a more transparent, effective and efficient way. She is also Head of Research at the Management Consultancies Association in the UK. Her books include *The Intelligent Client* and *Management Consulting in Practice: Award-Winning International Case Studies*. She is also the co-author of *Business Consulting: A Guide to How it Works and How to Make it Work*, published by The Economist.

François Rivard is a partner at Logica Business Consulting. He helps clients transform their organisations. He presents seminars and conferences throughout the year and teaches in French universities. He has written five books about information system management.

Logica Business Consulting is the consulting division of the Logica Group, a business and technology service company employing 39,000 people. It provides business consulting, systems integration, and outsourcing to clients around the world, including many of Europe's largest businesses. It is committed to long term collaboration, applying insight to create innovative answers to clients' business needs.
Logica Business Consulting has a network of 3,500 consultants located throughout Europe. Logica's consultants help drive the success of clients' transformation projects. They stand apart through their European culture, ability to work closely with clients, and unique blend of sector-based, functional and technological expertise.
More information is available at www.logica.com/consulting

www.maxima.fr

MAXIMA
LAURENT DU MESNIL●EDITEUR

192, bd Saint-Germain, 75007 Paris
Tél. : + 33 1 44 39 74 00 - Fax : + 33 1 45 48 46 88

© Maxima, Paris, 2010.
ISBN : 978284001 670 0

Table of contents

Preface

Twenty years ago, multi-million pound business consulting deals were something signed on the strength of a short slideshow and a handshake. And consultants rarely ventured beyond the boardroom. When their big ideas filtered down to the front line, they often turned out not to be fit for purpose. Processes had to be unlearned, redesigned and relearned, at a colossal cost.

No more. Today, clients rightly expect more for their money. They're not just looking for "thinkers" but "doers", people who can deliver measurable value and tangible results. People with real knowledge of different markets and cultures, and a global set of skills. Consultants have always needed relevant practical experience and innovative ideas, but today they also need to demonstrate a wider and more intimate understanding of the complex relationships between business processes, people and technology. From initial ideas, to managing operational improvements using IT, through to the final delivery and beyond.

To deliver real change, consultants also need the freedom to be creative. When purchasing departments start to get too heavily involved in defining the brief, they end up stifling the chances for serious innovation.

In this book, we take a fresh look at the client-consultant relationship from both sides of the table. It features contributors from across Europe, exploring the unique expectations and practices in different markets – and their best-kept secrets for getting the most from your business consulting partnerships.

Andy Green
CEO, Logica

I

Introduction

Mapping out a new client-consultant relationship

More from less: it will be the central theme of business in the 21st century.

Whatever type of organisation you work in, wherever you fit in its organisational structure, the people around you expect more from you than ever before. Your shareholders want better returns; your colleagues expect you to do the impossible; your employees look to you to set priorities and clear the way through the morass of everyday work in order to achieve what is important, not just what is urgent.

After decades in which organisations have sought to minimise their costs, the recent recession has taught us that, whatever costs you have cut, these will never be enough. Now, the still tentative economic recovery is teaching us that organisations have to deliver still more, of higher quality and with greater responsiveness, without allowing their costs to creep back up.

Management consultants play a crucial role, and one that has been steadily increasing over the last 20 years, as organisations become clearer about the functions and activities which are central to their long-term existence, in which they need to excel, and those which are required for only short periods of often intense activity. Consultants help clients in three fundamental ways. First and foremost, they provide specialist skills which can be crucial to a particular project or initiative but which are in scarce supply. Given sufficient time and money, other organisations can acquire these skills too, but if the skills are only required for a short time, then bringing experts in straight away saves time and ultimately money. But consultants also help create momentum. Trapped in the daily rhythm of work, reacting quickly to immediate problems, it can be hard for managers to find the time to work on new projects. Even when they can, their day-to-day commitments inevitably distract them. By contrast, consultants are accustomed to working on projects, rather than in line-management roles, and can focus all their attention on a longer-term initiative without being pulled in other directions by existing commitments. Consultants not only bring experience of past projects in other organisations – a map of the road, if you like – but the energy to push projects through to their conclusion. Last, but by no means least, consultants bring an outside perspective and are therefore able to look at an organisation objectively and challenge existing assumptions, whereas managers, however senior they may be, become caught up and constrained by the organisational norms around them.

Consultants and the organisations that bring them in can each make important albeit different contributions; their skills and ways of working are complimentary.

This brings us to the central thesis of this book: one of the ways in which organisations can get more from less is to leverage the knowledge and experience of consultants more effectively, but doing this depends on balanced co-operation between clients and consultants.

Much literature produced by consulting firms is given over to the term "working in partnership", but it has never been very clear what this means in practice. The whole concept of partnership has been misused to a point where, these days, it simply refers to the ability of two organisations to get along with each other. Clients don't want such "partners" anymore, because getting the best value from consultants depends on far more than this. As this book explains, it requires co-operation at all levels, from the individual to the corporate, and a structure in which there is an equal contribution from both clients and consultants.

Imagine you're going on a long car journey, through difficult, perhaps even un-mapped terrain. You can choose to make this trip by yourself, but the preparations will take longer and the travelling itself will be tougher. You will have no one to share the driving with, no one to check that you're on the right route. No one will make sure that you have everything you need for the journey and for your destination, except you. As the day of departure approaches, you'll get pulled in different directions. Have you checked the oil and the tires? Have you packed the things you'll need? Do you have the right maps? You'll also have no one to bounce ideas off or to help solve problems. What do you do when the engine fails? If you've gone off course, what's the best way back? Perhaps most importantly of all, if you're alone when you encounter a problem en route, you're far more likely to give up and turn back. Sharing the journey with others gives you extra pairs of hands, different skills (someone who knows how to repair the engine for example), and different suggestions when you encounter a problem.

People who travel together are more likely to arrive.

The same is true in business. The work of a senior manager in any organisation can be a lonely one; often it appears that those around you expect the earth from you. Bringing in additional support – consultants – for a specific journey makes sense. But what you don't want is someone who is pleasant to talk to, as they sit in the front seat of the car, but who doesn't share the driving, help read the map, or pack the luggage. Interesting conversation may be entertaining but it doesn't help get you to your destination. Having decided that you need help, you need real, practical, tangible help.

This book uses the metaphor of a journey to explore what that more meaningful client-consultant relationship looks like.

Part 1 (**Spark**) looks at the issues you need to consider when planning the journey.

The first chapter (**Knowing where you want to go**) explores in greater detail why organisations use consultants. When organisations decide to hire consultants, they typically focus their attention on the project or problem at hand. They might need an IT system replacing, or they might want someone to review the operational efficiency of their HR function; they might want help gathering data to support a difficult decision, or need advice on how best to manage the disruption involved in outsourcing their finance and administration. What they do not always think about is why they require external assistance at that point in time. What is it that the consultants will do or bring, that the organisation cannot do for itself?

This is the equivalent of deciding whether you want to make the journey by yourself or with others. You may decide that, because it is a short journey through familiar country, that you don't need any help. You may identify people in your own organisation who can share the driving with you, or who can read the map. Or you may conclude that, because you're travelling through unchartered territory and because your own staff are already very busy, you need some people to travel with you. Once you've decided you need support, the next question is the kind of support you need. Crucial to getting the best out of any consulting project is having a clear idea from the outset about what it is that the consultants can do that you cannot do for yourself – their *differential* value. Do you want specialist skills, or a road-map and the energy to help you complete your journey more quickly and successfully than would be the case if you were travelling by yourself? Or do you need an external perspective, someone whom you can trust to be independent?

The answers to these questions will determine the kind of consulting firm you should choose to make the journey with you. As Chapter 2 (**Choosing the right travelling companion**) explains, there is no point selecting a small, specialised firm if you're looking for help in maintaining momentum in a large-scale project, or asking a firm that facilitates change if you want detailed analysis of an external market. Recent changes in procurement have made it more difficult for clients to debate their exact needs with potential suppliers, but it is crucial to do this if you want to ensure that you're using consultants, not only where they are absolutely necessary, but also where they can add the most value.

In Part 2 (**Engine**), we will turn our attention to what you need to do just prior to the journey, to ensure you get to your final destination as efficiently and successfully as possible. We will focus on three critical areas here:

• Chapter 3 (**Shaping the ecosystem**) focuses on how you establish an "ecosystem" in which clients, consultants and – where they form part of a project – hardware and/or software providers all co-operate. This is the foundation of a successful relationship.

• High-level commitment and sponsorship is the theme of Chapter 4 (**Building commitment to the journey**). It is pointless to expect people who work with the consultants, to be fully committed to a project if they do not think the people they work for are. Thus, every time a senior manager fails to come to a steering group meeting sends a message to everyone else that the organisation does not really take the consulting project seriously. Ensuring top-level commitment depends on the early involvement of those concerned and realistic planning. However, it should not be seen as a one-sided affair: the consulting firm needs to be equally committed and some type of performance-related pay may contribute to this.

• In Chapter 5 (**Creating the metrics for success**) we look at how both sides need to invest time and effort, even before a project has started, defining what success will look like and finding the appropriate set of metrics with which to monitor and evaluate the project a as whole.

Part 3 (**Acceleration**) tackles the issues you need to address during the journey – during the course of the consulting project itself – if you're to arrive at your destination as efficiently and successfully as possible. Here, we will consider five critical points of leverage which will ensure you get the maximum value out of using consultants:

• The more difficult the journey, the more vital is good communication. **Ensuring transparency** (Chapter 6) looks at the importance of open communication within the consulting ecosystem. Internal people need to understand why consultants have been brought in, if they are to work effectively with them, otherwise they tend to feel marginalised and undervalued. Yet most communication during a consulting project comes from the senior executive who decided to hire the consultants and his or her immediate team. Not all of it filters down to people who work alongside the consultants. Indeed, a law of inverse proportions works: the lower down in the project hierarchy an internal person is, the more important it is for them to be able to work with the consultants effectively, but the less likely it is that the top-down rationale for using the consultants will have reached them. To resolve this, the sponsoring executive needs to send out a clearer message, aimed at all levels, on a purely consistent basis. Without this clear and consistent centre, reminding everyone of what is at stake, there is a risk that the ecosystem will fall apart.

- Unexpected problems are encountered in every journey, however well-planned they may be, and being able to respond and get back on the road quickly is essential. Chapter 7 (**Being innovative; being flexible**) examines what people mean when they talk about innovation in consulting projects. Clients should expect consultants to bring new ideas, but these can take many forms: insights into their business, a willingness to be flexible and tailor their approach to fit the client's unique set of circumstances, or better, more efficient ways of working. "Innovation" doesn't have to mean grandiose ideas which are supposed to revolutionise the world. However, where it does, play a vital role is in ensuring that the consulting firm can explore alternatives. When the road is blocked ahead, a firm's ability to think on its feet and be creative in practical terms will be profoundly important.

- Clients typically hire consultants to help them solve issues, but this should never result in long-term dependency. It is therefore important that consultants make **Sharing the driving** (Chapter 8) a priority, passing on their skills and experience in order to build the clients' own. But sharing skills does not happen by accident: consultants bring different skills – specialist know-how, an ability to engage people in a professional manner and their experience gained from helping other organisations solve similar problems – and passing them onto the people they work with requires careful planning. This chapter identifies four main barriers to sharing skills effectively, ranging from lack of time to organisational complexity, but also puts forward concrete ways in which the knowledge consultants bring can be passed on.

- Chapter 9 (**Engaging everyone's enthusiasm**) looks at an aspect of the consulting ecosystem which most people don't think about: the extent as to which the individuals from the client side, who work with the consultants during the project, stand to gain from its successful conclusions. Consultants themselves are usually highly motivated to succeed: this is, after all, their job, plus they have the advantage of not being distracted by other work so staying focused is easier. Moreover, many firms will only promote consultants who can show their clients are satisfied, so doing a good job has economic and career advantages as well. By contrast, employees can feel alienated by the presence of consultants, as though their employers are sending out the message that they are more prepared to listen to consultants than their own employees. To counteract this, it is important to consider how those people involved in a project from the client's side can benefit from it, whether that takes the form of acquiring new skills, accessing new opportunities for promotion or simply having the chance to meet senior people. Any project, whether it involves consultants or not and however well-planned it has been, requires people to go the extra mile, to put in discretionary effort above and beyond that which the project plan commits them to. For consultants, this is simply part of their job, but internal people need a reason and incentive to make it part of theirs as well.

• Chapter 10 (**Travelling together**) explores how clients and consulting firms should work together. There is little point, if you're travelling to the same destination, in taking parallel tracks. The balanced co-operation on which the consulting ecosystem is based is not just a function of structure and governance, but goes straight to the heart of how the different contributors to a project – the travellers on the same journey – operate. All sides have to co-operate: one is not imposing the solution for a specific problem on the others, rather everyone is working together towards a common goal. But co-operation still has to be balanced: it does not involve one side going along with a strategy someone else suggests in a sycophantic fashion, but means you treat people just as if they were part of your team.

Part 4 and Chapter 11 (**Managing international projects**) looks at the specific challenges involved in managing international consulting projects. Detailing the differences between countries' approaches to consulting, it identifies four distinct types of international consulting projects, each of which has strengths and weaknesses. The key to success, therefore, is to ensure that the right type of project is used in the right circumstances.

Two over-arching points emerge from all this material.

The first is that, in the consulting ecosystem, the same rules apply to all sides. Thus, clear communication is not just something that you should demand from your consulting firm, but something you should also expect internally. Similarly, consultants are less likely to be committed to a project if they believe that their client isn't committed to it either. "As you sow, so shall you reap", we're rightly advised.

The second point relates to the difference between "doing the thing right" and "doing the right thing". The first is a process point: it is the means to an end, not the end in its own right, yet it is extraordinary how often this becomes the focus of all attention and effort in business. We define what our job entails and we get on with it, perhaps without regard as to whether or not our job is actually achieving what our organisations needs. For example, the software supplier implements a new system, fitting it precisely to the agreed requirements and delivering it on time and within budget – but without considering whether it will, in fact, do what the organisations wants. Similarly, the consulting firm defines the scope of its work, then focuses on delivering a perfect result, but within the confines set and ignoring broader problems. The client refuses to put in more effort than they agreed; even if they are aware that a small amount of additional help would increase the chances of success, they may demand that their suppliers make up the short-fall. "Doing the right thing", by contrast, refers to acting in support of the ultimate objective of the project: you know the contract says one thing, but that doing another is the right thing to do. "Doing the right thing" is not, in fact, just about contracts and process: it is an outlook, a compass for the journey, if you like, always correcting your course to true north.

A year or so ago, a multinational company carried out a survey about why consulting projects over-run. Like most other organisations, much of the consulting work they bought was paid for on a traditional time and materials basis, so the company was spending (or losing) considerable sums each time a project went on longer than expected. In trying to answer the question, they talked to a wide range of organisations, some buying consultancy, others consulting firms themselves. "Clients think we're trying to deceive them," said the consultant, "but they don't put in the time and resources we've told them they need to contribute. I worked with one client team who never did any of the actions assigned to them during our weekly project steering group meetings. After a while we stopped asking them to do anything because it was pointless and you can't tell a client off. Yet, when the project over-ran, they claimed it was our fault."

As Machiavelli rightly observed more than 500 years ago: "A prince who is not himself wise cannot be wisely advised... Good advice depends on the shrewdness of the prince who seeks it, and not the shrewdness of the prince on the good advice." In other words, you do not get to be an effective and intelligent client because the consultants and other advisers you work with make you one; rather, you use consultants well because you are already a good, "shrewd" client.

That is the heart of our book.

Part 1
SPARK:
PREPARING FOR THE JOURNEY

1
KNOWING WHERE YOU WANT TO GO

It's first thing in the morning. Double espresso in hand, you stride purposefully down the corridor for a meeting with your business unit's human resources team. The subject is talent management: how can you identify the people with the highest potential in your business and what can you do to nurture their skills? It is an issue that has been on the agenda for a couple of years and you are aware that your head office has one such programme in place, although you are not convinced it will meet your specific requirements, nor – if you are quite honest – are you really sure what it involves. However, the whole subject has been thrown into relief by the economic environment. You would have thought that a tough market would have made it easier for you to retain your best people. It has certainly made it easier to retain people in general but it certainly has not stopped two people, whom you had marked out for early promotion, from quitting in the last month nor one of your competitors from trying to poach your head of operations. So, as you enter the meeting room, you are aware that, this time, you really need to get something done.

Your HR director is flanked by two of his most senior colleagues. Already on the case, they have put together a presentation high-lighting the failings of the status quo. So why, you ask, if the business case for action is so compelling, haven't we managed to put a programme in place before now? The HR director shifts uncomfortably: it's partly time, he explains. His team is already fully-stretched and being able to dedicate resources to this is difficult. He's also not sure that they know enough about best practice in other organisations: the last thing he wants to do is waste time repeating others' mistakes. Finally, the director points out, an area such as this is clearly very sensitive: he doesn't want any of his team accused of being subjective or biased. These are all reasonable points and you start to see where he's going with this: should we bring in some consultants, you ask.

A changing way of doing business

Conversations like this are happening every minute, in every type of organisation. The last 20 years have seen enormous growth in the use of consultants to the point where it is now hard to find a Fortune 1000 company or major public sector organisation which does not use them, and on a regular basis at that. Several factors have driven this:

- Economic growth: Because consulting is something organisations choose to buy – unlike an audit, they do not have to buy it – it grows fastest when profits are high and the rate of return on investments looks positive.

- New technology: The last 20 years have seen successive waves of technology wash over business. Taking advantage of these innovations has required specialist, often scarce skills.

- Globalisation: Multinational companies tend to make greater use of consultants than national ones, partly because they have more complex, cross-border issues to resolve, but also because they encounter different competition and have to be able to respond.

- Recruitment freezes and labour inflexibility: Organisations turn to consultants for short-term resources, often when they cannot recruit full-time employees either because they do not have the budget to do so, or because the skills they are looking for are especially scarce.

• Changing management philosophy: The last two decades have seen significant shifts in our ideas about how organisations should be organised. In particular, we no longer expect even the largest corporations to do everything in-house: functions and processes have been outsourced to specialist service providers, whether that is an advertising agency, a cleaning company or a strategy consultancy. Managers no longer expect to do everything themselves; instead, they can tap into a reservoir of expertise outside the boundaries of their own organisation.

While this explains why the consulting industry has grown, why do individual organisations use consultants? Why, for example, does the HR team described above want to hire consultants?

Your first reaction – if you are the executive described at the beginning of this chapter – will probably be that this is an easy question to answer: you want the consultants to help your people establish a process for identifying and nurturing the best people in your organisation. The problem with this answer is that it is too high level: it focuses on the service to be provided ("talent management") rather than on what the organisation wants to achieve and why it cannot achieve this without external help. To use our analyse of a journey, it tells you what the car will do, but not where you want it to take you.

What do you want to achieve?

Organisations which are considering bringing consultants sometimes confuse the means and the end. They focus on the skills the consulting firm has and the outputs of the project they are working on, not on the business outcome those skills and outputs are intended to deliver. In our example, it would be a mistake for the managers of the company to think they are buying a talent management programme: they are buying a better way to retain and develop their managerial stars. This is the end they are seeking, and talent management is simply one of the means by which they may be able to achieve this end.

The starting point should always be your business objective: the place where you want your journey to end. Even this may not be as easy as it sounds: you may be clear about where you are trying to go, but your colleagues may not; they may even disagree with your end point. Such differences of opinion and approach need to be ironed out before you even think about hiring consultants: if the people who matter in your organisation are not in complete agreement about what you are trying to do, it is more than a little unfair to expect the consulting firm to deliver much in the way of value. From the consultant's point of view, there is little more frustrating than working in an organisation where you receive conflicting messages about what is expected from you.

Once you are absolutely clear about what you are looking to achieve, only then should you start to think about what the key components of your approach should be. For instance, you may decide there are several aspects to retaining and developing your best staff: a systematic assessment process which everyone accepts as fair or an executive MBA scheme onto which your high-flying staff can go. You may need to change the way you run your annual appraisal process. Your existing HR systems may need to be upgraded. You may also have to work with senior managers to change the way they treat their staff. Whatever components you identify, you should always remember that these are a means to an end, not ends in themselves – and you need to make this clear to the consultants you use, should you choose to use some.

Why do you need external help to achieve this?

The service a client wants and their decision to use consultants to provide it are two quite separate issues. If we simply think about consulting in terms of the service provided, we will never really grasp why consultants are necessary, and, if we cannot work this out, we will never get the best possible value from them. We need, instead, to consider the *differential* value that consultants bring – the things that consultants can do that organisations cannot do for themselves. To use our journey analogy again: every organisation could – eventually – get to their chosen destination, but it may take years and considerable effort to do so. Consultants may help them get there more quickly, more comfortably, and more safely.

Go back to our talent management example and ask yourself why it is that the HR team thinks they cannot do this work by themselves. The HR director gives three answers: he thinks that his team lack expertise and knowledge in this area and are already so busy that they cannot take on this extra work. In fact, the HR director is citing the most common underlying reasons why organisations bring consultants in.

Knowledge

Around half of all consulting projects happen because the client organisation lacks the specialist skills to do a specific piece of work. A bank that wants to set up a customer contact centre will hire a firm that specialises in this area. A university that wants to review its operational efficiency will turn to someone who has experience of doing similar projects.

Consulting firms are huge repositories of knowledge, but it is important to know that they have the knowledge you need and do not already have. Your starting point should be finding out what your organisation knows: the bank that wants to set up a customer contact centre may discover that one of its businesses in another country has already done this and be able to learn from that experience. If you cannot find it, the next question is how best you can acquire it. You could decide to hire a full-time member of staff with prior experience in setting up contact centres, but the right person might be hard to find and prohibitively expensive to recruit. You could decide to train one of your existing managers in this area, but that is not always practically possible and may take too long. When you have exhausted these possibilities, then – and only then – should you turn to a consulting firm for help. The specific – differential – knowledge consulting firms bring usually falls into one of five categories:

1. Technical skills – specialist areas of knowledge in specific fields.

2. Rigour – a highly disciplined and systematic process to collating and analysing information.

3. Cross-sector experience – a firm's ability to identify valuable parallels across different sectors, such as applying Lean manufacturing skills to public sector processes.

4. Global experience – the ability a larger firm has to pull together information from different countries.

5. Network effects – the extent to which a firm can put you in touch with other organisations or individuals who may be able to help.

Process and project management

Many clients know what they want ("talent management"), but they do not know how to implement it. Such organisations look to consulting firms to provide a clear road map that takes them from where they are today to where they want to be in the future. Sometimes, also, they see a benefit in using a consulting firm that can supply a dedicated team of resources to give the project the energy and momentum to ensure it will be completed on time. Consultants can focus all their attention on a specific project in a way that regular line managers, pulled in different directions by a multitude of objectives, cannot. Process projects account for around a third of all consulting and are the fastest growing reason why organisations use consultants – a testimony to how difficult organisations find execution.

As with knowledge, this reason for using consultants has several aspects to it:

1. Flexible labour – consulting firms can field dedicated teams to work on a specific problem very quickly. For clients that struggle to free people up from the existing jobs, whose resources are already limited, or who are reluctant to take on full-time employees perhaps because of economic uncertainty, consulting firms provide short-term assistance.

2. Experience of similar projects – the ability to draw on lessons learnt elsewhere in order to help clients avoid common pitfalls and emulate best practice.

3. A tried-and-tested methodology – where a consulting firm has had extensive experience of a specific project or issue it may codify that to provide clients with step-by-step guidance.

4. Technology and other assets – a consulting firm may be able to help clients manage their work through the better use of technology and other tools.

People, perspective and politics

While consultants may bring with them specific knowledge and methodologies, the way they work and their role as outsiders can provide value in its own right.

Clients can, over time and with effort and investment, acquire technical skills comparable to those of a consulting firm. They can set up their own internal consulting function which brings many of the process and project management advantages of a consulting firm. But the thing they find hardest to do is to be able to look at their own business with sufficient detachment. A consultant is an outsider who can challenge accepted assumptions, communicate ideas effectively, and help build consensus over difficult decisions. In our example, the HR team might find themselves in an awkward position, caught between business units pushing their own candidates forward for the new talent management programme. In such a situation, a consultant will be the neutral judge: someone who can bring an objective viewpoint.

In this respect, consultants offer:

1. Softer skills – perhaps in communication or facilitation, which help organisations deal with difficult issues.

2. Change management – acting as catalysts or helping people deal with periods of turmoil.

3. An outside perspective – the ability to see the wood for the trees.

4. A holistic view – an ability to see an organisation as a whole, not as the sum of separate parts (which is how internal managers tend to see it).

5. Unbiased advice – it is almost impossible for internal people to be objective because they have built up friendship and spheres of influence, and because they will inevitably have projects and initiatives they favour.

In summary

At a time when almost every large-scale organisation is making unprecedentedly extensive use of consultants, it is important to stand back and question exactly what your objectives are, and how a consulting firm may be able to help you achieve them in a way that your own organisation cannot. If you think it is appropriate to use consultants, be absolutely clear how they are going to help you:

- Are they going to bring specialist **knowledge** which your own organisation does not have and which it could not acquire relatively quickly or cost-effectively?

- Do they have **process and project management** strengths, based on a breadth of experience and flexible resourcing your organisation cannot match?

- Will they send **people** with the personal skills, **perspective** and professional detachment to help organisations deal with difficult times?

Being completely clear about why, at this fundamental level, you need the input of consultants, is the bedrock to the effective use of consultants. As we will see in subsequent chapters, it will help you select the right firm to work with, ensure that your staff work effectively alongside the consultants and understand the value that has been added once the project has been concluded.

Case study

EXAMPLES FROM THE UK

Clients hire consultants because they lack specific skills or knowledge internally, either in a particular sector or in resolving a particular issue.

At the British Council, Clare Withycombe, recalls: "We were looking for an experienced consultant who had experience of applying career management within an IT solution to help us address the development needs of our 8,000 employees worldwide, we did not have this unique combination of career management and IT skills in-house. Professional credibility was also important: we used consultants who were thought leaders in this sector and who would know what had worked – and what hadn't - elsewhere."

But clients also use consultants as an extra pair of hands, because their own people are just too busy. "The key issue for me has been bandwidth," says Simon Short at Vodafone. "Using consultants buys us time and space. There are lots of things we would like to get done, but if we really want to change something or think about something differently, then we have to create the opportunity to do so."

Using consultants for short-term input is a testimony to the growing complexity of business and specialisation of labour in the economy as a whole. However, it is undoubtedly also the result of many years of cutbacks and structural change in organisations. Bob Dench ran Barclays' investment management businesses and is now on the board of AXA: "Why didn't we use our own people? Because there was no fat left in the organisation. We'd taken the business through several intense efficiency exercises and we did not want to recruit permanent staff for short-term work. Such an approach also enables organisations to turbo-charge their businesses with short bursts of very high-level expertise."

Another valuable contribution consultants make is to bring an external, independent perspective to the many intractable problems facing managers today. At Prudential, Gary Gordon would never use consultants lightly. "I'm not a big fan of using consultants to determine the direction or strategy of your business," he says, "but, if you are going to be a successful organisation, you need to recognise your strengths and weaknesses, especially when it comes to making significant business decisions. Consultants are helpful when they provide you with another perspective on

.../...

your business. You can bring them in, in an advisory capacity, to ratify your plans rather than create them, to introduce subtle changes because they have a wider range of experience they can draw on. A good consulting team will help you challenge your assumptions."

Robert Sternick does not particularly care for consultants either. However, when his company, Infast, faced difficult decisions about sourcing its products overseas rather than making them locally, with the potential loss of hundreds of jobs, consultants provided valuable support: "In such situations, everyone internally has their own preference and it becomes difficult to separate facts from emotion. Consultants, as outsiders, can be neutral."

Momentum is important, too: "We didn't come with any baggage but could ask blunt and stupid questions which got to the heart of the matter," says Martin Haynes. "Sometimes people make themselves believe something can't be done. They give themselves all the reasons why they can't do it, but not the reasons why they can."

2
CHOOSING THE RIGHT TRAVELLING COMPANION

When you decide to go on a journey, who would you want to go with? Do you ask someone you know who has already made that journey? Do you choose someone you're comfortable with or someone who can drive the car fast?

If you're looking to bring consultants in to help you have to ask yourself similar questions. Do you:

a) Chat through your requirements with the senior partner of a firm over dinner or at the golf course?

b) Adapt the terms of reference you wrote for the last set of consultants and email it to some firms you found in Google?

c) Consult, perhaps rather grudgingly, someone in your central procurement team in order to send out a detailed invitation to tender to a long list of firms your organisation has worked with in the past?

d) Refer to your intranet for a very short list of preferred suppliers?

In this chapter, we will explore how the process of buying consulting has changed in recent years, highlight some of the drawbacks of those developments and put the case for an alternative approach.

A brief history of consulting procurement

Very few of you would have ticked answer (a). The chances are that, if you work in a big organisation, the way in which you buy consulting services has changed dramatically over the last ten years. In the first place, much more consulting is bought by many more people. Instead of being the preserve of the chief executive, around three quarters of all consulting projects are now commissioned by functional heads – IT, HR and operational directors – rather than Board members. For most organisations, bringing consultants in is simply a part of doing business: business requires more specialist skills than it did 20 or even ten years ago and they accept that it does not make economic sense to have every possible expertise available in-house on a permanent basis.

With more people buying more consulting, a typical organisation in the mid-1990s would have seen a terrific proliferation of the number of consulting firms it was dealing with. Certainly, the big brands and familiar firms would be there, but so, too, would be a whole host of specialist firms. That's still true for some organisations today: as many as 30 percent of you may have ticked answer (b) in our quiz. Your organisation may have well over a thousand different consulting firms supplying a panoply of over-lapping services. Your managers have *carte blanche* to choose the firms they want, so they use a combination of firms they have worked with before, firms their colleagues have recommended to them and firms (perhaps more specialist ones) they have identified through research, bumped into at conferences, or read about in newspapers. Although they may favour a particular firm, there is no real control on which they choose to use.

It is very difficult for organisations in this situation to control their expenditure on consultants. Indeed, they are very unlikely to know how much they spend. It was this which prompted many organisations, in the aftermath of the dotcom mania, to ask their central procurement teams to rein in spending. And it was the growing role of procurement, as much as the broader economic slowdown, that caused the consulting industry to contract in 2002. Trained in buying commodities, writing contracts and negotiating volume discounts, the procurement people raised their hands in horror at the way consulting services were bought. Their first action was to identify and track expenditure; their next was to try and reduce the number of firms being used. However, reducing consulting expenditure did not turn out to be as easy as reducing, say, the telecoms bill. Consulting covered a much broader range of services; it was difficult to compare one firm with another; pricing structures were opaque at best. Moreover, the relationship between the procurement manager and the end-users, the managers who actually needed the consultants, was fraught with tension. The latter bitterly resented interference in "their" job, did not believe that the procurement manager was qualified to help them decide which firm to use and delayed telling them about consulting projects for as long as possible. For their part, the procurement managers saw their clients as wastrels, willing to throw money on consultants without considering whether they had chosen the right firm or were paying the right price. Procurement teams reacted in one of two ways: either they became morose bureaucrats who would belligerently insist on taking their internal customers through an often byzantine purchasing process or they became "yes" people, so concerned about being marginalised in all the major buying decisions that they redefined their role as facilitator, ironically there to help managers spend. Indeed, these changes did not result in long-term or sustainable cuts in the use of consultants (by 2004, the industry was growing again by more than 10 percent a year). They did, however, result in some consolidation of expenditure: rather than having perhaps a couple of thousand consulting firms on their books, such organisations had only a couple of hundred.

If you ticked answer (c) in our quiz, and we think around 60 percent of you will have done so, then this is the situation you are in. If you want to hire consultants, you are expected to work with someone from the central procurement team. The person will not only want you to provide a business case for using consultants, but will have some views about which firm you should use and will try to encourage you to buy from a firm with which your organisation already has a framework agreement. But, from a procurement point of view, this situation is intended to be temporary, a state you pass through on your way to enlightenment. At the end of this journey, your organisation will have a preferred supplier list of perhaps ten firms at most and you will be expected to buy all the services you need from these firms because the quality of their services has been checked and their prices cut. Perhaps only ten percent of you have reached this point and would have answered (d) in our quiz because this level of control is hard to achieve and maintain. It requires a substantial commitment from those at the top of an organisation to set an example, so the chief executive's choice of firm is limited to preferred suppliers just as much as middle managers'.

The limits of formal procurement

If you ticked answers (b), (c) or (d) in our short questionnaire, your sense of whether this is the best way to buy consultancy will be determined by the quality and sophistication of the relationship between procurement people and end-users in your organisation. Some of you will have a helpful, well-informed and responsive procurement team and a good choice of potential suppliers. But others will see their procurement team as an obstacle to be overcome, making their life difficult by insisting that they adhere to a rigid set of rules and preventing them from using consulting firms with which they are familiar.

However, it is important to realise that procurement people have an unenviable task, because the nature of consulting does not easily lend itself to conventional, more formalised purchasing techniques. They face three key challenges: lack of standardisation; unequal information; and the extent to which the quality of service received depends on the interaction between client and consultant.

Every consulting project is different

Almost all the tangible products we buy as consumers are regulated in some way, but services are different. Some services are regulated: the more essential the service and the less choice we have about whether we do or don't buy it, the more likely it is to be regulated. Thus, the training and accreditation of doctors and dentists is taken immensely seriously, but that of hairdressers is not. At the furthest end of the discretionary scale is management consulting. For example, there are usually no legal reasons for implementing a new customer relationship management system, although there may be a valid, urgent and excellent business case for doing so. The level of regulation is therefore entirely at the discretion of individual consulting firms: there are no professional bodies to which individuals or firms must belong and no qualifications management consultants must have. Some firms try to compensate for this by developing their own training programmes: a software company may accredit consultants in its implementation process; indeed, the more a firm would like to position its services as must-haves, rather than nice-to-haves, the more likely it is to have developed some type of internal regulation.

Regulated products and services are unquestionably easier to buy than unregulated ones, because regulation creates standardisation. But the problem with consulting is that it covers a very broad range of activities and that every project is individually designed to meet the unique needs of a particular client. Indeed, the problem is not just that standardisation would be difficult, but that it would also be counterproductive. Research by American academics suggests that the value of management tools and techniques lies in the way their application is tailored to the needs of a specific organisation and that the more such a tool becomes a standard process, the less value it is likely to add.

This has implications on how you buy consulting. Standardisation may make a procurement manager's life easier, but it will impair the value of the consulting service from an end-user's point of view. Where a product or service is standardised, nothing you do in the purchase process will affect its quality. Aggregating demand for photocopying paper does not mean you end up with poorer quality paper; getting a volume discount from a car manufacturer for your fleet does not mean you end up with substandard cars. When it comes to buying a non-standard service, the quality of what you receive can be dramatically impacted by the way you buy it. Negotiate a consulting firm down too hard on rates and you will not get their best people on your projects.

Asymmetric information

When buyers and sellers have unequal levels of information, prices and quality fall. Prices come down because buyers cannot test and do not trust the quality of what they are buying before they have bought it: because they do not think the quality will be what they have been promised, they ask for a discount. Quality falls because suppliers cannot afford to invest or innovate, as they know they will not recoup the money spent. So, over time, the bad drives out the good. High quality goods or services, which customers are not prepared to pay for, are replaced by poor quality, but cheaper ones, creating a vicious circle in which expectations, quality and prices continue to fall.

This phenomenon, which economists call information asymmetry, is one of the key threats to the consulting market. Client confidentiality, which is sometimes justified, but more often is driven by an unwillingness to admit to problems, stops many consultants from being able to talk about their work. Clients may not have access to enough information on the skills and experience of the individuals they are about to hire. They also find it extraordinarily difficult to measure the value of the services provided (a point to which we will return in the next chapter).

In practical terms, this makes it very hard for end-users and procurement managers to judge the quality of the consulting services they are being offered. Each side reacts in a different way. End-users fall back on gut instinct, exactly the approach which a decade of more formal procurement has tried to eradicate. Procurement managers respond by placing undue weight on the small number of attributes which are possible to measure and compare from firm to firm, such as size, number of consultants and/or offices and, of course, price. Neither approach provides a particularly satisfactory solution.

A good working relationship

The final complication in the process of buying consulting is that good consulting depends on the client as much as on the consultant: consulting does not happen in isolation. When you talk to clients who have been involved in highly effective consulting projects, where the results exceeded their expectations, the factor to which they typically attribute success is the sense of partnership between the client staff and the consulting team.

The exact nature of this partnership is something we will be exploring in much more detail in the next section of this book, but it is worth noting at this point that this critical ingredient to consulting success is also very hard to judge when you are buying consulting. Every firm will claim to "work in partnership" with their clients, to promote "effective team working" in the project and will cite clients who say that the level of integration was such that they could not tell where their team finished and where the consulting team started. Such words are easy to say but hard to prove. You can speak to the firm's other clients, but a relationship that worked for them may not suit your organisation. Moreover, the team you work with may be slightly or completely different, so how will those dynamics affect your working relationship?

Again, end-users and procurement people are polarised in their response to this problem. End-users rely on a sense of personal chemistry: do they think they will get on with the consultants at a personal level? Procurement managers will look for lists of skills and qualifications. While each approach has its merits, neither will give a real sense of what it will be like to work with someone in practice. Both take place in the artificial environment of the buying cycle, when everyone is on their best behaviour.

Creating a dialogue

These three challenges – non-standardisation, lack of information and the importance of working relationships – make consulting a peculiarly difficult service to buy. While recent developments in procurement practices have been designed to remove some of the weaknesses of the purely personal approach, they are not the whole answer. As well as these approaches, each of which has benefits, you also need a process that tests out what it will be like to work with the consulting firm in practice, a process that, as far as possible, replicates a real working environment with all its tensions, strains and expectations. Clearly, you cannot do this with your original long list of firms, so the standard techniques outlined above play a role in whittling down the firms you might want to work with to perhaps two or three. It is then with this much smaller number of firms that you need to explore how you will work together.

So, what should you do?

Ask the remaining consulting firms to work with you, and with each other, on one of the initial areas of the project. Let's suppose that you want to put in a new performance management system, one that cuts across your organisational structure, forcing managers in all areas to take a more disciplined approach to carrying out annual appraisals and recording individuals' objectives and performance. It is the kind of project that may well meet resistance along the way as successful implementation will involve changing behaviour as much as systems. You could invite the – let's say – three consulting firms which have got through your initial procurement process to come to a workshop. Put them in a room together and present the situation, as honestly and openly as you can. Talk about the way in which managers are accustomed to working and ask them to work with your staff and each other to develop an approach which will ensure this crucial constituency will co-operate. Use this to assess how the firms perform under pressure and to find out how comfortable you and your staff will feel working with the individual consultants. It is also reasonable to assume that, if the consultants can add value during this period, they will be able to do so during the actual project.

You may meet some resistance from the consulting firms themselves:

• Although keen to win your business, they may be reluctant to talk about their approach in front of their competitors, saying this is part of their competitive advantage. You can be reasonably demanding here: a good consulting firm will be quite prepared to share their thinking, at least at a high level, because they know that a theoretical approach is only part of the solution and that success depends on tailoring their standard approach to meet your needs. But do not expect them to hand over their entire methodologies.

- Some firms, especially small specialists, may not be able to afford to do this free of charge. The best way to deal with this is to ensure that the process is not drawn out over too long a period. Choose an issue which the consulting firms can debate, research and come up with suggestions within two or three days. Expect the firms to work hard during this time, but do not expect them to work for free any longer.

- The consulting firms will be concerned that this activity may lengthen what may already have been a lengthy sales cycle. Delays are, in fact, bad for both sides. Because of the way they are designed, most consulting firms find it quite hard to balance supply and demand and having consultants not occupied on client work is very expensive. If you delay your decision, there is a danger that the team the firm proposed get moved onto a different project where the client has already given the go-ahead, especially if the consultants involved are particularly good. This is another good reason for keeping this competitive workshop swift and self-contained.

It is worth noting that this approach will not just help you identify the people you can work with most effectively. As the buying of consulting has become more formalised, it has become harder for end-users to develop their requirements. Go back to the short quiz we had at the start of this chapter: option (a), which happens less and less these days for many good reasons, had the advantage of giving the client and consultant an opportunity to debate exactly what was needed and how best to go about it. That dialogue is harder to maintain in a world of more formal procurement. The distance between end-users and consultant may be greater – the procurement manager may be a gate-keeper or, at worst, a barrier. The terms of reference for your project may have to be established at a very early stage in the buying process, limiting consulting firms' opportunity to challenge them and your ability to adjust them.

By creating a competitive dialogue – the chance for a small number of consulting firms to debate your requirements with you and for you to test out the all-important personal chemistry between you – you will dramatically increase the value you will get from using consultants.

In summary

Recent changes in the way in which organisations buy consulting services have resulted in more formal purchasing processes. While these have improved the degree of control organisations have over their expenditure in this area, such processes have three limitations:

- They work best when applied to standardised purchases: every consulting project is different.

- Buyers and sellers have unequal amounts of information making it hard for the former to judge quality and the latter to prove it.

- A good relationship between the person using the consulting services and the person who provides them is critical to success in consulting. Most formal procurement processes do not take this vital aspect into account; at worst, they may create barriers to establishing it.

Overcoming these challenges involves creating a genuine dialogue between clients and consultants before the contract is signed. This can be done by asking a short list of firms to work with you, and even each other, for a small number of days, so that you have a real opportunity to evaluate not only the quality of the work they produce, but also the quality of relationships they can forge.

Part 2

ENGINE: GETTING READY TO GO

3
SHAPING THE ECOSYSTEM

Although much of this book will be focused on the bi-lateral relationship between client and consultant, often at a personal level, it is important to stress two things from the outset. The first is that, increasingly in consulting as a whole, but particularly where technology and business consulting are concerned there are often three parties involved: the client organisation, the consulting firm and technology hardware and software suppliers. The second is that relationships between all these parties also have to exist at a corporate level: it is not enough for individuals to get on, if their organisations don't.

Although we might be tempted to represent this three-way relationship as a triangle, it is both more productive and accurate to consider it as an ecosystem, in which the work of each participant overlaps and where the success of the whole is dependent on them all working effectively together (Figure 1).

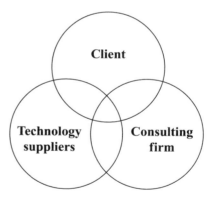

Figure 1: The business consulting ecosystem

Ecosystems survive and thrive on mutual co-operation. Far more than the "partnership" arrangements often talked about in consulting projects, ecosystems require not only mutual respect and equitable commercial arrangements, but an environment in which all the participants benefit from the presence of the others. Indeed, everyone needs everyone else. Clients clearly depend on the consulting firm and technology suppliers to provide the skills, the momentum, and the hardware and software they need. Consulting firms can help clients map out their requirements and implement complex new systems, but they need input and time from the client in order to do that (to understand what they really want and need, for example). Obviously, consultants have nothing to implement if the technology firms don't supply it. However, the technology firms need help specifying what is required, as well as dealing with the complex problems that typically go hand-in-hand with large-scale projects. After all, the business of technology suppliers is not consulting, anymore than the business of consultants is to build hardware and software, or the business of clients is to do things which are not part of their core business.

The rules of an effective ecosystem

That's the dream: so how do you make it a reality?

Respecting the boundaries

In an ecosystem, every participant has their place, and everyone else knows what it is. The best journeys are those in which the work involved is shared between different people, each of whom is better than the others at their particular tasks. The car driver does the driving; the map-reader makes sure they get to the right place by a reasonable route; the person who is best at packing should have made sure that nothing is left behind but that everything is packed in the minimum number of cases; and so on. Each task is treated equally: there's no point in driving to the wrong place, reading a map for the sake of it, or getting to your destination only to discover that you've forgotten half your luggage. Arguments happen only if the map-reader tries to snatch the wheel, or the driver insists on packing his or her own case, or if the luggage-packer insists on a different route.

The same is true in the consulting ecosystem. We all know that clarity of roles and responsibilities is hugely important, but perhaps we're not always willing to live within the boundaries these establish. How many projects have we all been involved in, in which people cannot resist the temptation to interfere or have an opinion about an area they are not directly involved in – and perhaps don't even know much about. Indeed, it's particularly tempting because within the ecosystem there are always two sets of people who are not experts in an area. To go back to the car analogy: it is easy for the map-reader to sound knowledgeable about driving a car to the person who packs the luggage because neither of them (at least in our simple scenario) know how to drive the car as well as the driver does. Similarly, the driver and the map-reader can voice strong opinions about the poor packing to each other, because they didn't have to do it – if they had, they might well have done a worse job. It's always easy to sound like an expert when you are looking in from the outside and especially if you have someone else on the outside to talk to.

Not taking sides

This leads to a further point about the consulting ecosystem. Three is often an uncomfortable number: "two is company, three is a crowd" is an old English proverb. Where there are three sides, one side always runs the risk of being isolated. If they raise a difficult question or challenge an assumption, there is always a danger that the other two sides will close ranks. This means that, in any interaction between three groups of people, it is hard to get people to be honest, particularly about problems. No one wants to question the status quo.

Yet, because no project ever runs entirely smoothly, it is essential that issues and obstacles are flagged up as soon as they emerge. Most can be resolved with early intervention; few if you ignore them until the last possible minute.

It is therefore crucial that the governance structure of a project be set up in such a way that it encourages open and honest communication. Some of this is cultural: people who want to challenge what's going on need to do so in front of everyone else and bring evidence / experts to prove their point. Some of it is commercial: it should not be possible for any side to gain financially from the discomfort of the others. But, underlying all of this, you need to ensure some degree of independent oversight: a fourth in some of the conversations who can neutralise the potential for conflict. This might be made up from people from the client organisation, the consulting firm and the supplier who are not directly involved in the project; alternatively it could be the most senior person from each organisation. The crucial element is that they have the ability to act as a group, not side automatically with their own organisation but to listen to the evidence presented.

Owning and solving problems collectively

The clear demarcation of boundaries should not, however, prevent the three players in the consulting ecosystem from being able to work together when problems – inevitably – arise.

Suppose our car, carrying the driver, map-reader and luggage-packer, gets a flat tire. The first reaction will probably be to blame someone else: the driver might argue that the map-reader took them over roads which were too rough; the map reader might retaliate by saying the driver wasn't looking where he was going, and so on. Attaching blame doesn't just waste time in often pointless recrimination; it also usually means that one person is left to solve the problem (because they're to blame). If the driver loses the argument, he'll be the one left to change the tire.

This is equally true in consulting projects. The first approach of everyone in the ecosystem is to blame one of the other groups because they don't want to bear the cost and upheaval of rectifying the problem. If a scapegoat is found, everyone else can sit back and enjoy the spectacle: fun though that may be in the short-term, it almost certainly means that the problem takes longer to fix or isn't fixed properly, creating long-term problems for everyone. It takes time for the driver to put the new tyre on and he may not make a good job of it. Pooling the collective expertise of everyone else would have speeded up the process and ensured a better result. Indeed, sometimes, you have to call in an outside expert (the equivalent of a car repair company), because none of the participants in the ecosystem know how to fix the problem. Don't automatically assume that, because one group or company caused the problem, they are the best ones to resolve it.

Of course, that doesn't mean that you should not spend time working out what the root cause of a problem was: doing this is the only way of guaranteeing the same issue won't reoccur. But such analysis is better undertaken once the immediate problem has been resolved.

Owning and exploiting opportunities collectively

Much of the literature on making business-to-business relationships work focuses on the negative side: the "stick" that has to be in place in order to force compliance, rather than the "carrot" which encourages it. While obviously not very motivational, the real problem with such arrangements is that they create a situation in which individual participants in the ecosystem are incentivised to act in their own interests, rather than in the interests of the ecosystem. Imagine for a second that our car driver, map-reader and luggage packer were each going to get a bonus for doing their job particularly well. Clearly, they will put their own job above the combined effort: the luggage-packer may spend extra time packing and re-packing, meaning they are late getting to their destination.

Some of the best examples of consulting ecosystems are established in such a way that new ideas and innovations can be pooled and openly discussed while also being acknowledged as having come from one party. A simple record is kept of who originally thought of the idea and the benefits it yielded. At the end of the project, the benefits that accrue from them can, once realised, be split between the collective group and the organisation or team which first thought of them.

The ecosystem "contract"

What all this amounts to – and can be encapsulated in – is a form of social contract which each of the three groups – clients, consultants and technology suppliers – agrees to adhere to and which governs their behaviour for the duration of the project. You don't need a lot of words to do this, let alone lawyers drafting complex documents, just a simple statement of how you expect people to behave.

But of course, contracts only matter if someone is prepared to enforce them and if there are meaningful rewards for "good" behaviour and penalties when people behave "badly". And it is here that the relationships between companies matter more than the relationships between individuals and it is also here that the facets of a successful ecosystem, outlined above, become more than just nice words to say.

There are three crucial aspects to this:

- **Governance:** The relationships in an ecosystem, in contrast to those in a traditional prime-sub-contractor arrangement, are equitable. This does not mean that each party has an equal amount of work to do but that the success of the project depends equally on each party carrying out their role to the best of their ability. One party may have a relatively small amount of work to do, but it is just as critical to the project as a whole as every other part – something that needs to be encapsulated in the contractual arrangements. Moreover, to avoid the difficulties in communication and collective ownership, outlined above, that stem from there being three participants in the ecosystem, the commercial arrangements also need to establish a governance structure in which there is a fourth "party", providing oversight and/or arbitration is required. Ideally, this is made up from very senior people from each of the three organisations.

- **Transparency:** No ecosystem can function if those involved are not open and honest with each other. The idea of open-book accounting, in which every side in a contract has a chance to inspect the accounts of the others, is already commonly-accepted practice in large-scale IT and outsourcing projects, but it typically only extends to the two biggest participants (the client and the prime contractor). In an ecosystem, the same principle has to be applied to all those involved. Furthermore, transparency is not simply a question of letting others see your numbers: the financial metrics are just the starting point for a discussion about the economics of the project. The mutual respect, which is a fundamental to an eco-system, stems in part from the acknowledgement that everyone should gain from it. The client clearly gains by having the project completed to their satisfaction, and on time and budget. But the commercial arrangements also have to allow the suppliers to make a profit: driving down costs to a point where they cannot make what to them is an acceptable margin will almost inevitably compromise the quality of the service provided. Once "an acceptable margin" has been agreed at the start of the project, each participant should also be able to highlight issues – perhaps as the result of something that one of the other participants is doing – that may reduce their margin.

• **Outcomes:** Rewarding each supplier individually encourages them to act in their own interest, so a fundamental aspect to the contractual arrangements surrounding an ecosystem is to ensure that part of their payment depends on the overall success of the project, as defined in terms of the client's business objectives. Thus, it is not enough to say that the implementation of a given system, or the outsourcing of a particular function, constitutes success. Success comes only when the new system or the outsourcing contract delivers the benefits sought by the client.

In summary

Large-scale consulting projects are often structured as bi-lateral arrangements, with the main contract being between the client organisation and a single, lead supplier. Other suppliers, consulting firms and software companies for example, may be involved, but their role is subordinate to the main supplier. However, such arrangements don't take account of the extent to which a project's success may be dependent on the contribution of other suppliers. A better way to think about such projects, is as ecosystems where the governance structure, extent to which information is shared between those involved, and payment all support the collective endeavour.

4

BUILDING COMMITMENT TO THE JOURNEY

It seems ironic to be talking about commitment. Surely, when you decide to go on a journey, perhaps taking your friends or family with you, all you need is a decision, some planning – and then you're off. Yet how many of us have been on journeys in which disagreements emerge? Many of those disagreements start in the front of the car: an argument about the best route or perhaps the driver doesn't really want to go and his or her grudging attitude communicates itself to the restless children at the back.

Similar things can happen in consulting projects. They start off in a blaze of activity and enthusiasm only to run out of steam part of the way through. Asked why this is, clients often cite the equivalent of the reluctant front-seat people; that their colleagues or bosses were not really behind the consulting project, that they did not give the impression that it was a priority. This communicates itself to the consultants too: as they battle to get time in people's diaries (always a crucial test of commitment), they lose faith in the project. And that creates a vicious circle which is hard to break free from: people in a client organisation are far less likely to be fully behind a project if they don't think the consulting firm is either.

A typical situation?

Dieter works at the head office of a major German retailer where he's responsible for strategy for the group as a whole, a mixed bag of different chains in Western and Central Europe. Acting on the suggestion of his boss, the Group chief executive, Dieter has been investigating what can be done to create a better culture of customer service. Service isn't poor, but Dieter would be the first to admit that, given a choice between serving a customer and going into a stock room to check inventory levels, most store managers would opt for the latter.

After much thought, Dieter has brought in a consulting firm to help him. He suspects that the general managers of all the chains could benefit from some external input, and this consulting firm specialises in the services sector and has worked with many firms Dieter views as leaders in customer service. By sharing their expertise and experience, he is hoping to change people's perceptions, inspire them by giving them examples from other organisations so they take customer service more seriously. At the same time, Dieter is aware that many of the general managers of the different retail chains are suspicious of interference from head office: "They don't think people like me have a real job to do," he complained recently to his immediate boss. "We can advise and recommend, but we don't have that much power. The general managers are the real decision-makers in their organisations: what they say, goes, not what we say."

Let's think about what happens next. In the first scenario, Dieter brings the consulting firm in, and develops the brief with them. He asks them to work closely with the general managers of each retail chain to establish a small joint client-consultant team to identify a small number of key changes they could make in their stores to make their staff more customer-centric. Each chain will have a different programme of activity, reflecting their different cultures and consumer markets.

"Not another head-office initiative!" explodes Joachim, the general manager of a Dutch music retailer and an accountant by training, when he reads Dieter's email. "Every week, there's another bad idea coming out of Frankfurt: HR, marketing, knowledge management, new budgeting processes, new expenses policy." His management team shake their heads in sympathy, when he breaks the news to them later that morning. "That's what we have a head office for," quips one, "to burden us with pointless extra work while we're struggling to keep our heads above water." Immediately, almost everyone round the table starts to find reasons why their best people need to stay where they are, leaving the HR director to find a couple of reasonably willing volunteers, whose input will be supplemented by a group of people from various parts of the business. Anna is one of these: running the store in Utrecht leaves her little time for something like this, but she sighs and emails back that she can make the first meeting.

A week later, huddled into an airless meeting room down the corridor from Joachim's office, the HR "volunteers", and assorted people from different parts of the music chain look expectantly at the consultants, waiting for a road-to-Damascus-like experience which will explain to them why they have been pulled out of their busy day jobs at the behest of a remote and bureaucratic head office. The consultants, for their part, are struggling to understand just why the enthusiasm in the room is at such a low ebb.

Top-level sponsorship: the start of everything or nothing

Behind every consulting project is one person, the person who initially decides that consultants are necessary, who steers the selection process and who ultimately signs the cheques once the work has been done. But of course it is never as simple as that.

Typically two problems arise.

The first is that, although the role of sponsor should be a single person, many organisations split the role of the sponsor between several people. A director may decide that consultants are necessary, but asks one of the people who reports to him to select a firm and work with them. Because the manager to whom this task is delegated was not party to the decision to bring consultants in, he may disagree with it (everyone can be upset when they feel excluded); more simply, they may not understand exactly what the director wants and give the consultants a misleading brief. The opposite also holds true: a middle manager may believe that using consultants is the right thing to do and, through persistence, has persuaded her boss to agree. The boss, having never been completely convinced that this money should be spent, is a bit more reluctant to put effort into the project. Alternatively, an organisation may decide that a whole group of people is the de facto sponsor, even though such steering committees are rarely effective or efficient decision-making bodies.

The second problem has to do with seniority. Because people often talk about top-level commitment, they think it has to be at the most senior strata of an organisation as possible, thinking that has been reinforced by the higher levels of sign-off which have been required for consulting projects during the recession. However, senior people are often too far above the operational issues many consultants are asked to resolve and are too busy to commit much more than lip-service to any given project. Often, they end up delegating by default not design, the worst of all possible worlds.

The solution lies in:

Ensuring that the decision about whether or not to bring consultants in is made after the project sponsor is appointed. This way a single person is responsible both for the project and the effective use of consultants, if there are any on the project. It should not be the case that the decision to bring consultants in makes the organisation belatedly realise that a project sponsor is needed.

Taking away some of the work and commitments the sponsor would otherwise have had. Organisations tend to assume that it is possible to pile almost limitless amounts of work and responsibility on its most senior people, creating an environment where – inevitably – the urgent but unimportant tasks crowd out the important but less urgent ones. Rather than allowing the sponsor to delegate, he or she should be taking some of their existing tasks and temporarily handing them over to their second-in-commands so they have time to concentrate on the project.

Commitment from the sponsor's colleagues...

Almost everyone in an organisation mimics the behaviour and attitudes of the people above them: that is not the result of self-serving ambition so much as simple human nature. A chief information officer I once talked to recalled being asked to cut costs (again) and, finding that there were few costs which could be cut, questioned how much time was wasted in the organisation as a whole on the "governance" of other departments. To calculate this, she worked out where she and her immediate colleagues were spending their time, on the basis that however they apportioned their time, you could be sure that the people who reported to them would do the same.

It therefore follows that, if you bring consultants into your organisation and you want their work with you to be a success, then you have to ensure that everyone at your level and above agrees with that decision and is publicly prepared to help. If they are not committed, you can be sure that the people working for them will not be either. Clearly, the same would be true of an internal project, but consulting projects are peculiarly exposed to this risk; perhaps because they involve outsiders who people may resent; perhaps because the consultants themselves are less familiar with the politics of the organisation and are therefore less able to help themselves; perhaps because it is often a single person's decision to bring consultants in, not a team's.

There are two main ways to ensure you get top-level commitment: you involve them in the arrangements for the journey at the earliest possible stage, and you are clear about what you expect from them on the journey itself.

Early involvement: One of the main reasons why people are reluctant to commit to anything, let alone consulting projects, is ignorance. In this example, Joachim's reluctance to get involved is not just motivated by his views of the head-office, but by the fact that the subject matter is not familiar to him. So what could Dieter have done differently? For a project of this scale, scope and importance, it would have made sense to involve the general managers, not simply in the decision to bring consultants in, but in the discussions around what could be done and how to approach the issues. Given the subject matter, it could also have made sense to take the general managers to visit companies with a more embedded culture of customer service, so they could get different views, from fellow business people, of the importance of the project and the impact it could have on their business.

Clear and realistic planning: Explaining what you are going to get from a consulting assignment, and when, is not just important in simple project management terms. Senior people know from bitter experience that many corporate initiatives fizzle out from lack of support. Especially in the public sector, there can be widespread cynicism about whether a new initiative is being announced for political reasons and little expectation that things will change in practice. To counter this, you have to persuade people that your project is different, that once begun, it will be finished – and the best way to do this is to set out some clear, straight-forward and achievable goals. Yet it is extraordinary how many Dieters there are who, egged on by their ambitious bosses and buoyed by their own optimism, do not do this basic groundwork.

...At all levels

But commitment is not something confined to the top of an organisation, although many managers, especially senior ones, tend to think it is.

Once you have ensured that the senior people in your organisation are setting an example, publicly and practically supporting the consultants you have brought in, the key obstacle to commitment at other levels tends to be logistical rather than motivational. In our retail group, only the HR department has freed up its staff to work alongside the consultants, by getting someone else to do their job for the duration of the project. For Anna and the other people who have been pulled rather unceremoniously out of their daily jobs, their ability to commit to the project relies on how easy it is for them to find people who can take their place, even for short periods of time. In this scenario, it is more than likely that attendance by these people at the meetings organised by the consultants will gradually wane, especially since any return for them from the extra effort may not be clear in the short-term. This becomes a vicious circle, with the consultants, anxious to take the project to conclusion, increasingly filling the spaces vacated by people who have been pulled back to their line management roles. Indeed, it is not impossible that, by the end of the project, what began as a joint client-consultant team, will have become a wholly consultant one – something that will have a negative impact on its ability to change the culture of the retail chains.

Dieter should have put more thought into how general managers such as Joachim would select participants and give them the time to contribute in practice. He could, for example, have provided the funding for interim managers who could have back-filled the jobs of these volunteers for the project. Such a move would have had the added benefit of sending a message about the importance of the project and that, if offered the choice, the Group expected its employees to put customer services first.

...And from the consulting firm as well

Because the consultants working on a project are highly motivated to complete it (their career progress, as well as asense of job satisfaction depend on it), clients rarely think about how to ensure that they, too, are publicly committed to success. Economic downturns typically trigger renewed interest in paying consulting fees on a performance or risk-reward basis. With budgets for new projects drying up, it is logical for organisations to look for alternative ways to fund the things they want to do. Yet, for all the talk, only around a tenth of all consulting projects are paid for in this way. There are good and bad reasons for the relatively low-take up. Clients often feel uncomfortable agreeing to too large a reward and are unwilling to experiment. Despite its name, risk-reward is often perceived to focus on transferring risk, rather than rewarding good performance.

Where risk-reward is used, it may be for the wrong reasons. A client who is uncertain about the value the consultants will add on a particular project may choose this approach, not because they want to ensure a consulting firm's commitment to a specific goal, but because they want to avoid paying for a project that might fail. You have to ask why, if they are concerned about failure, do they not either do something to increase the probability of success or cancel the project entirely. Equally, where a client is completely confident that the consultants will succeed, there is little incentive to create a bonus structure that effectively rewards them for doing their job. One of the ironies of risk-reward deals is that they are therefore more likely to be used where the chances of success are low.

Moreover, although risk-reward deals are often touted as a means of aligning the objectives of customers and suppliers, there is a real risk that they will do the opposite, driving a wedge between them as they argue over the minutiae of who is responsible for what.

The term risk-reward covers a multitude of sins, but can be categorised in three ways:

- Carrot or stick? Here, the focus ranges from the negative ("If you don't achieve X, we will not pay you Y.") to the positive ("If you achieve X, we will pay you Y.").

- Standard fee or bonus? Meeting a target may simply entitle a consulting firm either to a "normal" fee, typically calculated on a time and materials basis, or to some type of bonus.

- All or part? Many consulting firms are willing to put a proportion of their fees on the table, perhaps as much as 20 percent. In such arrangements, the firms effectively invoice for their costs during the project but have to wait until its satisfactory conclusion before they earn their profits. However, a minority of firms are prepared to put their entire fees at risk, much as lawyers are prepared to work on a no-win-no-fee basis.

There are, however, several problems associated with risk-reward projects. They can be expensive: clients who put a risk-reward deal in order to reduce the price they pay may be in for a shock: risk-reward is not necessarily a way to get something done more cheaply. They can be hard to implement: people typically underestimate the amount of work involved in setting up a risk-reward deal. You have to develop a business case, evaluate the possible scenarios, sell the concept to almost-certainly cynical colleagues, and that is all before you start measuring and tracking the benefits the consultants should be delivering. Risk-reward requires a greater investment of people's time than that of conventional contracts. It is difficult to measure the benefits: because of the variables involved, it is almost impossible to link the outputs to the work of the consultants. Furthermore, because the benefits are hard to measure and attribute, the temptation is either to rely on metrics that are too simplistic and generic to be useful or to become trapped in endless negotiation. Finally, they can encourage the wrong behaviour. We all know that metrics and targets have a direct impact on what people do – and this applies as much to risk-reward work as it does to any other area of business. Suppose you have a team of consultants implementing a new IT system whose payment depends on ensuring it goes live on a specific date: they are more likely to cut corners in order to meet that deadline. They will act in their own interest, not that of their clients.

So, what are the most important lessons when it comes to applying risk-reward payment structures to consulting projects?

• Be clear about what the consulting project is trying to achieve: Don't start from the assumption that risk-reward is the right approach.

• Don't expect risk-reward to be a panacea: It is a poor substitute for good management.

• Don't use risk-reward as a substitute for picking the right firm: One of the reasons why organisations consider risk-reward is that they are concerned their objectives and those of the consulting firm they are working with are not aligned, but in these circumstances they would do better to pick a firm whose internal metrics and culture support what they're trying to achieve. Consultants paid bonuses for selling more work will inevitably focus on that; those who know they will only get promoted if their client satisfaction ratings are high will concentrate on delivering a good service.

• Focus on large-scale, long-term projects: For risk-reward to work effectively, the potential bonus for a consulting firm has to be big enough for it to feel the risks are worth taking.

- Define the type of service you are buying: The two key deciding factors are the level of ambiguity involved and the extent to which the consulting does (or does not) have control over the outcomes. The more discrete work is, the simpler the problem and the more static the circumstances, the more appropriate risk-reward becomes.

- Measure what you want to be managed: Most risk-reward work focuses on project-related metrics such as deliverables, budget and timescales. While important, these will inevitably tend to focus the attention of the consulting team on the means, not the ends. It may be more effective in the long-term to connect the consultants' work with the way in which they work and/or the business benefits.

- Identify metrics you can measure: In a risk-reward deal you have to be able to measure success, but defining appropriate measurements may not be easy.

- Consider alternative risks and rewards: If your aim is to provide a consulting firm with the motivation to perform above and beyond what the contract specifies, there may be better ways to achieve this than conventional risk-reward. Financial reward is not everything.

But the other factors in ensuring a consulting firm is publicly committed to the success of a project come back to the client organisation. As a client, think about your internal metrics: the success of using risk-reward depends on having a clear and meaningful set of metrics which can be accurately monitored. It is much easier to do this in an organisation where measuring and managing overall performance is important. Lastly, it is worth remembering that commitment from either your colleagues or your consultants will never work where the relationship you have with them is adversarial. Perhaps the single most important lesson learned from consulting failures and successes has been the recognition that commitment is a collaborative effort.

In summary

Many journeys start off well but finish badly because the people on them were not completely committed to them at the outset. By contrast, even the most difficult journeys can be finished successfully where all those involved are determined to make the best of things. The commitment of anyone on a consulting project – sponsors, senior executives, middle managers and even consultants – cannot be taken for granted but has to be systematically and deliberately established:

- Sponsors should be appointed before the decision is made to use consultants, not afterwards, and they need to be able to hand over some of their existing workload in order to give a project the attention it deserves.

- Senior executives are best won over by involving them at the earliest possible stage in the "journey" and by having realistic plans which clarify how much time and effort will be required from them.

- Middle managers and other people who work side-by-side with the consultants on the project will be pulled in several directions if there is not a proper plan for carrying out their usual work in their absence. It can make better economic sense to hire interim managers to "back-fill" internal managers' jobs so they can work with the consultants than to bring in more consultants.

- Performance-related fees may not be appropriate for every consulting project, but they can be a useful demonstration, internally as well as externally, that the consulting firm is willing to put its money where its mouth is.

Case study
THE SCOTTISH GOVERNMENT

The Scottish Government is the devolved government of Scotland. It is responsible for all devolved policy matters in Scotland including Health, Education, Local Government, Transport, and Justice. The Scottish Government provides professional Civil Servants to support the 129 member Scottish Parliament.

Since the mid-1990's, the Scottish Government has contracted with a commercial partner to assist them by providing specialist services broadly described as "Systems Integration" (SI) services, which comprise Integration Services, Verification Services, Technical Assurance Services, Technology Refresh Services, Technology Design and Performance Management Services

In August 2005 Logica was successful in winning a contract to provide these services for the ensuing five years. Speaking about the contract, Anne Moises, Chief Information Officer and contract owner at the Scottish Government, said: "Ten months after awarding the new contract to Logica I can say with confidence that we made the right decision. I was greatly impressed by the smooth and seamless transition of the core service in the early days. But since then I have been even more impressed by the way Logica has embraced and responded to our evolving business needs."

Anne summarises: "I am delighted that we have so quickly reached a position where we understand each other's objectives and our combined strengths – which are significant. We are now moving forward a number of customer-focused shared services initiatives using 'mixed economy' teams and deploying complementary skills from our two organisations [......] I do believe we have a proper partnership relationship with Logica. I believe there are significant opportunities for us to work together to improve the delivery of public services over the coming years."

5

CREATING THE METRICS FOR SUCCESS

In 2007, the UK's Management Consultancies Association surveyed organisations to see how many of them attempted to measure the value delivered by their consultants. Almost 60 percent said they did not do this. Among those that did, there was no consensus about the best way to do it, although most relied on project-related metrics. Had the firm completed the project on time? Had it kept within its original budget? A minority had tried to measure the satisfaction levels of the people the consultants worked with.

Should we be shocked? Perhaps: but we should not be surprised.

One of the maxims of business is that only what gets measured gets managed. Irrespective of the economic conditions, every project where there is an element of choice involved needs a business case. Everyone needs to justify their expenditure by having a positive and prompt return on investment. The greater the degree of choice, the more important the business case will be. Unlike, say, an audit and certain types of legal advice, the extent to which a particular consulting project is required is up for debate. An IT department that is under pressure to cut its IT costs is likely to see the expert input from a consultant who knows about consolidating data centres as essential, but the finance director who is responsible for watching every cent expenditure may not. Equally, the finance director who wants to use consultants to assess the viability of an HR shared services centre may find himself in conflict with an HR director who cannot see why it needs consultants to do this. A water-tight business case cuts through such conflicts by reducing the decision to a simple go / no-go response.

But if a business case is especially important for a consulting project, why is it that organisations seem so lackadaisical when it comes to measuring the value they receive? Chapter 1 made the case for having a clear and unequivocal view about why consultants are necessary. Chapter 2 argued that conventional procurement approaches – old and new – need to be supplemented by a competitive dialogue, the chance for a small number of consulting firms to test your assumptions and for you to test their credentials. Both these approaches will help ensure that the consultants you work with add value, but to be able to manage, monitor and maximise that value, you need to know exactly what it is.

The barriers to measuring value

There are three fundamental reasons for this contradictory state of affairs: the first relates to the way in which business cases are written; the second to the inherent nature of consulting; and the third to human nature.

Anna is a (fictional) head of a sprawling government department. Sitting behind her desk, in one corner of her spacious, high-ceilinged office, she feels slightly cut off from the day to day operations of the organisation. She suspects (and rightly so) that the information she sees has been filtered through many layers of the hierarchy. Copious yet beautifully-crafted papers are tabled at carefully managed meetings. Not a word is out of place.

This creates a problem: with major cutbacks in expenditure on the cards, Anna is concerned that her staff are quietly vying with each other to protect their own particular empires, identifying savings everywhere except in their own backyards. In such circumstances, it's hard to get an objective view, which is why she fingers the report on her desk doubtfully. The idea of combining the finance function of the main department with that of several satellite organisations in order to create one service centre, capable of dealing with the needs of all the organisations, makes perfect sense. Economies of scale will be greater; the quality of service will be more consistent and professional, at least once an initial period of upheaval is passed. Investment is needed, for new systems and to re-engineer processes. Outside help is also required: a software company to install the new system. But, with such a strong overall business, Anna feels there is room to include help from a consulting firm: officially, this will be to oversee project management and to work with her staff to ensure they have the skills they need; unofficially, the firm will also be her eyes and ears on the project. She can't afford to let such a high-profile initiative fail because of internal rivalries and departmental politics.

A year later, the transition to the new shared services centre is well under way. True, there have been teething problems, but that's only to be expected in such a vast and complex piece of work and the services centre is already starting to save the department money. Success breeds success, so Anna has had several meetings with other departments which are now anxious to go down the same path. She goes over the business case with them. Excellent, they say, but tell us about the consulting firm you used, what did they do? Anna gives the official line, but also hints that the firm has been helpful in sorting out some of the sensitivities inevitably involved in a project that cuts across all the activities of the department. Yet, some of the people she meets are sceptical about this: perhaps their business cases are less robust and they want to know the consultants are really necessary. Suddenly, Anna finds herself hard-pushed to put a value on their contribution...

Anna's experience illustrates the three reasons why organisations struggle to measure the value of consulting when they can measure the value of so much else:

- **The business case:** Like most organisations, Anna's team has developed a business case for the project in its entirety, including the use of consultants. In the initial stages of a project, this can seem to make sense, but it subsequently makes it much harder to pinpoint the specific value that consultants add.

- **The nature of consulting:** Measuring the value of consulting is not as easy as it sounds. A project may start out with clearly specified terms of reference but change during its course as new issues come to light. Do you measure simply the project itself or the business objectives you want to achieve? Some projects are more intangible, and therefore harder to quantify than others, which makes it hard to benchmark return on investment or payback period. You may be using external advice to identify cost savings but planning to implement the recommended changes yourself. What is the value created in this case? Pinpointing the potential savings does not actually save you money; moreover, you may find that savings on paper do not translate into savings in practice. Over how long a period should you measure the benefits? A hike in productivity from working with consultants may turn out to be short-term as old, less efficient habits re-emerge. Other benefits may take time to have an effect.

- **Human nature:** Anna's reasons for hiring consultants are perfectly sound, but she is understandably reluctant to discuss some of the management issues within her department, so she down-plays this aspect of the consultants' role. Human nature intervenes in other ways: because consulting is difficult to value, neither managers nor consulting firms want decisions to be exposed to too much scrutiny, concerned that, in conventional terms, the return on investment will look too low.

You could argue that none of this matters: the barriers to valuing consulting cause Anna a few moments of discomfort but nothing more. That would be to underestimate the ramifications of this problem. Most of our purchase decisions are based on an assumption of value. We continue to buy washing powder because we know it makes our clothes cleaner; we buy a bicycle because we know that riding will make us fitter; we go on a holiday because we know that we'll come back to work feeling refreshed. Consulting, of course, is a much bigger purchase than all of these: if we cannot be sure of the value it adds, then we will probably buy less of it over time. Obviously, that is a worry to consulting firms looking to grow, but it is just as much of a problem for organisations that need to access the specialist expertise a consulting firm has or to rely on consulting firms to help them complete projects more quickly and successfully. If they cannot access those resources, their business will suffer.

Overcoming the barriers

So what could Anna have done differently?

In the first place, she could have insisted on having two business cases. There should have been one for the project itself, based around using her own staff to manage the project, not the consulting firm. Clearly, for this to be an honest assessment, Anna should have had a frank discussion with the different parts of her organisation about how realistic the timescales and estimated benefits were and what they would be dependent on. She would then have been in a better position, not only to understand where the consultants would have been able to add value, but also to assess what that value was likely to be. She could then have asked for a second version of the business case to be written, this time including both the costs and benefits of using consultants. The difference between this one and the first business case would have helped her isolate the incremental value to be added by using consultants.

The second problem to solve is deciding exactly which metrics to use. It is tempting to say that every consulting project should be measured differently but that ignores the fact that there are common elements to the work consultants do and the value they add. In Chapter 1, we identified three fundamental reasons why organisations use consultants: knowledge; process and project management; and people, perspective and politics. Each of these has distinct benefits, and those benefits can be valued:

- **Knowledge** helps organisations make better decisions. By learning lessons from elsewhere, you are better able to avoid the pitfalls into which other organisations have fallen. Better information helps you take a rounded view and can give you the confidence to make a tough decision.

- **Process and project management** helps you execute plans or implement systems more effectively and more efficiently. This, too, can take several forms: you may mitigate risk more comprehensively or make better use of the resources available to you; using the experience of the consulting firm, you may be able to plan and prioritise more effectively

- The independent **perspective** and change management skills of the **people** involved may leave you with more capable managers and more effective teams.

Having had a debate about why the consultants were needed, Anna could have looked to measure their contribution accordingly. She was using consultants for all three reasons: for their knowledge; for their ability to increase the probability that the project would be a success; and for the way in which they could help her team to work together more effectively. In dealing with the questions from her colleagues in other departments, she could have therefore talked about the extent to which the consultants helped her and her staff:

- **Take better decisions:** What would have happened if they had made different, poorer decisions and how much would this have cost the department?

- **Execute more effectively and efficiently:** If the consultants had not been there, would the department have been less likely to complete the project on time or realise the expected benefits? What would have been the opportunity cost of delay?

- **Work together more effectively:** Anna's hidden agenda was to ensure that the shared services project did not come to grief as the people under her argued about how it affected their business units. This is perhaps the hardest aspect to manage, but potentially is the most valuable aspect of the work the consultants did because managers who are working well together are much more likely to be able to take better decisions and execute them more effectively and efficiently. Again, the key here would have been for Anna to contrast what might have happened if the consultants had not been involved and to measure the impact that would have had on the project as a whole.

The third and final difficulty Anna faces is that she is doing all this in retrospect. Had she asked for two business cases before the project had been commissioned, and had she discussed with the consulting firm how the department planned to measure their input before it started, she would now have little difficulty in articulating the value the consultants added.

In summary

Most organisations know they should measure the success of their consulting projects but few do so rigorously in practice, for three reasons:

- The costs of consulting are usually rolled up into an overall business case, not evaluated separately.

- The value of much consulting is inherently difficult to measure.

- Managers are unwilling to have their decisions scrutinised.

To overcome these problems, organisations that use consultants should ensure they develop two business cases: the first covers the project itself and focuses on the outcome the organisation is looking for; the second analyses the way in and extent as to which consultants can help achieve that outcome. They should also identify metrics which match their requirements.

Creating metrics for success

Measuring the performance of a consulting project remains an exercise which is often customised to the content of each project and prepared contextually by the client and the consulting firm. Beyond evaluating adherence to timelines and the quality of deliverables, new indicators emerge in order to facilitate co-operation between the two parties and to rectify certain performance deviations. The facts presented below are taken from various consulting assignments carried out by Logica Business Consulting teams.

The quality of collected data is key to the effectiveness of a consulting assignment. The process of preparing this data collection is of crucial importance. The ratio between the number of people invited to participate in interviews and the number of people who have openly co-operated may be an indicator of the quality of information obtained and become a means of qualifying the success or failure of an assignment.

Other qualitative factors on the content of workshops can be put forward: coverage of responses obtained, participation rate of experts, average time for validation of reports...... these tools markedly improve the management of an assignment.

As regards assignments linked to the integration of technological innovations in an information system, ratios such as the agility rate or integration coefficient quantify the impact of these innovations on the existing system. Although the measurement of such ratios is sometimes subjective, they provide differentiating elements which help the client to grasp the main concepts.

Metrics must take into account performance elements and financial indicators, mainly when it is a case of establishing the benefits gained by the business as a result of the consultants' actions. Thus, an assignment carried out on behalf of a major British retail bank underlined the benefits of real-time monitoring of payment flows and immediate alerts for handling payment irregularities. Reduction of late payment penalty amounts, prevention of customer attrition: profits demonstrated a return on investment right from the first year.

Part 3

ACCELERATION:
PUTTING YOUR FOOT DOWN

6

ENSURING TRANSPARENCY

"If there's one thing I would go back to and change if I could, it would be to spend more time telling people what was going on. The message has to be consistent; it has to ring in everyone's minds." This is how clients typically describe one of the most important factors in determining the success of a consulting project. The comments hold true today; ironically, in a world of over-communication, they are truer than ever.

Stephen is a (fictional) project manager for a large consulting firm who, over the years, has built up an excellent working relationship with International Water, a utilities company. But today the circumstances are different. Sitting uncomfortably in IW's atrium, he's here to meet Joel, the new CIO and CIO of Global Electricity, another utilities company that has just successfully concluded a hostile take-over of IW, its archrival. But the animosity stirred up by the bid is nothing compared to the acrimonious relationship that Stephen knows to exist between Joel and IW's outgoing CIO, Paul. It is Joel who has hired him now, because Stephen knows the IW systems department so well; but he is also acutely aware that Paul may well see him as a traitor.

Although hurtful at a personal level, Stephen's main concern is the impact that might have on the job he has to do. Joel has asked him to review the progress and costs of IW's ERP implementation, a project that Paul has spear-headed. This will involve interviewing Paul's staff, most of whom are fiercely loyal to him and resent Joel's presence. They will also be frightened for their own jobs and think Stephen is there to assess their capabilities, so getting an honest picture will be hard. On top of all this, Stephen is rightly concerned that Joel is out on a limb, claiming to other members of the Global Electricity Board that he can make significant savings by axing parts of the project and ignoring their concerns that cutbacks will delay the project and compromise the benefits it ultimately delivers.

Thinking through the difficult meetings that lie ahead, Stephen bites down on his one remaining fingernail.

The barriers to transparency

Perhaps you think this is an extreme example. It is not common, admittedly, for a consultant to be trapped between two people who regard each other with such naked enmity. But consultants often do find themselves trapped in a tangled web of relationships, in which their ability to do their job properly depends on people who are suspicious of their motives.

A large part of the solution lies in transparency. People who do not know why consultants are there are much more likely to:

• Resent them ("What have they got that I haven't?")

• Question the contribution they may make ("I don't see what value the consultants add.")

• Feel marginalised ("Why doesn't my boss listen to me instead of listening to the consultants?")

• Reject their recommendations ("I don't see what good that will do! It'll never work.")

In surveys, when you compare the responses from clients who were completely satisfied with the outcome of their consulting project, with those from people who said they were only partly satisfied, transparency is one of the areas of greatest difference.

Completely satisfied clients, almost universally, rate as high the consulting firm's willingness and ability to communicate openly and honestly; partially satisfied ones are much less likely to do so. The same surveys also give us a clue about the type of transparency required. Generally, senior people think that they and the consulting team have a completely transparent relationship; it's the people beneath them who tend to be much less positive.

From evidence such as this we can conclude two important points and infer a third:

• People who have been effectively communicated with are more likely to understand why the consultants are there (a point that takes us all the way back to Chapter 1, about ensuring you have a clear purpose in bringing consultants in). People who know why the consultants are there are more likely to measure the consultants' contribution correctly and are less likely to feel pushed aside by them ("I understand that my boss hired Consultant X because Consultant X has specialist skills and experience I don't have but which we, as an organisation, need at the moment").

• People who are lower down the project and organisational hierarchy are less likely to understand why the consultants are there because more senior people have either not communicated this information at all, or have communicated it ineffectively. Transparency does not always "cascade" well in an organisation.

• People who hire consultants know that transparency is important, and the bigger, more complex the project is, the more important communication is going to be. However, not unreasonably the focus of their efforts will be on explaining the project as a whole, not specifically the reason why consultants will be involved, that is something that, if they think about it at all, they will leave to the consultants themselves.

The four keys to building transparency

These are precisely the issues which Stephen, our long-suffering consultant, is confronting as he sits among the potted plants in International Water's atrium. It is likely that Joel, his new client, has sent an email around to Paul and his team, explaining the review process. Stephen's name will have been mentioned in the last paragraph but Joel will be leaving it to Stephen to explain why he is there. (If you have ever been a consultant, you will know that the first few minutes of almost any meeting when you are trying to gather information is spent doing just that.) Because Joel is not familiar with the organisational structure of International Water, his email probably only went to some of the relevant people; some will not have got it at all and will be relying on gossip. As a result, the chances of Stephen being able to do his job properly have shrunk considerably.

So what should he do? He needs to:

1. Persuade Joel to send out a clearer message, not just about the project but also about his, Stephen's, role in it.

2. Ensure the message reaches all the people involved in the project, however indirectly.

3. Stay on-message throughout the project, and ensure that everyone else does too.

4. Be open and honest about progress and feedback during the course of the project.

A clearer message

This is perhaps the easiest and most straight-forward aspect of transparency. The senior person in the client organisation who is ultimately responsible for the project (not the immediate project manager) needs to put together a clear and unequivocal statement that covers:

- Why the consultants have been brought in – in other words, what they can do that the organisation cannot, or does not wish to do itself.

- What the consultants are actually going to do (in Stephen's case, for example, it would be hugely helpful to explain that he and his team are *not* there to assess individuals' suitability and career prospects).

- How long it will all take, so that everyone understands that this is not a long-term arrangement and that they are not being marginalised.

- How they are expected to work with the consultants, that this is not (or should not be) a one-way process and what they should, as individuals, gain from this process. The latter is a particularly important point and one that we will return to in much greater detail in Chapter 10.

Too often, the person who has hired the consultants relies on the consultants to explain these points themselves. That never works, because comments from the consultants are much more likely to be seen as self-serving and an attempt to justify their presence. Moreover, if the consultants have to put their own case forward, it sends a subliminal message to the rest of the organisation that the senior sponsor is not willing to publicly justify his or her decision to bring consultants in – and if the senior sponsor does not think the consultants should really be there, no one else will either.

Getting the message to everyone who matters

Saying something is one thing: getting everyone to hear it is entirely different. As a client once put it to me, "you have to over-communicate so that everyone understands the situation. Just because you understand it, doesn't mean that others do."

In one sense, the issues here are no different to those that apply to corporate communications in general: you have to think about the language and medium you choose. But one of the most important mistakes both clients and consultants tend to make is to focus their communication on the upper echelons of management. This is particularly ironic because senior directors are likely to have been involved in the decision to bring consultants in and so they will already understand why the consultants are there and what their role is. In other words, most communication efforts are centred on the people who need it least.

There are two aspects to diffusing the message:

• **Depth of communication:** As with so much corporate communication, organisations rely on these senior people explaining things to their staff, who are expected to explain things to their staff, and so on, all the way down through the multiple layers of the organisation. This cascade approach works well where the organisation is good at communication, in the same way that water will pass through layers of rock providing that it is permeable. Quite obviously, that permeability – the willingness of middle-managers to pass on messages – varies hugely between organisations. In general, however, it is directly related to the extent to which the message, directly or indirectly, increases a middle-manager's ability to do their job or enhances their prestige and career prospects. Up-to-date information on an organisation's new strategy or an inside-track about a new initiative will clearly do that, but the advent of consultants is a more ambivalent message. Middle-managers may feel that their standing has been undermined or their voice in decision-making has been marginalised. The consultants, as outsiders, are not part of their team and are not under their control; if anything, they make middle managers look powerless. In this context, the cascade principle does not work: middle-managers become a barrier to effective communication, not an important channel.

This means you need to choose a means of communication that will reach all levels directly and equally.

• **Breadth of communication:** Senior managers who hire consultants often underestimate how wide an impact the latter can have. If only those immediately and directly involved with the project are receiving information about it, people elsewhere will draw their own, misinformed conclusions. Therefore, information on consulting projects needs to be spread more widely than information on internal ones. This is one of the most important reasons why consulting teams should be based for a significant proportion of time in their clients' offices. The old model of consulting, in which an adviser turned up, gathered data and then went back to his office to write the report is largely out of date. However, it is still worth remembering that a consulting team based in your office has many more opportunities to explain their role to people informally at lunch or the water-cooler, than one which chooses to work behind closed doors.

Consistent communication

In a project such as this, any slight discrepancy in the message being put across about the role of Stephen's team will be magnified and picked over by the people working for International Water. Any hint that the consultants are there to draw up a list of who stays and who goes will be seized on as evidence that there is a wider conspiracy at large. Similarly, any sign of disagreement between Stephen and Joel will be interpreted as proof-positive by Paul and his team that Joel is not qualified to replace him.

Actually, the biggest problem here is not the client – Joel in our example –, but the consulting team. Junior consultants are sometimes tempted to embellish their role to impress the people they work with; more senior ones may be accustomed to thinking on their feet, inadvertently tailoring the messages they give to different groups. It is therefore important to apply the same principles of communication to the consulting team, as it is within the client organisation, albeit on a smaller scale. Depth and breadth matter here too: every consultant on Stephen's team, irrespective of their grade or expert area, needs to understand the scope of their remit and be able to communicate it consistently to all the people they work with.

Being open and honest throughout the project

It's tempting to think that transparency only matters at the start of a project because that is when uncertainty and confusion tend to be greatest and where misunderstandings can have the biggest impact. However, transparency should not stop when the consultants start working:

- Each side should be open about the costs it is incurring in the project, whether these are more or less than expected. If the client is incurring more internal costs than he expected, is there something that the consulting firm could do to help? If the consulting firm is being forced to do extra work, can the causes be identified and more done by the people on the client side?

- Both sides also need to carry out simple but regular surveys of those involved in the project. Clients should question their own staff on the performance of the consultants, and the consultants on the performance of their staff; consulting firms should ask similar questions. All the data should then be pooled, allowing both clients and consultants to identify and resolve problems as they emerge. High-level results should be available to everyone involved in the project, however junior; if nothing else, this creates peer-pressure that drives up performance. Where serious issues are uncovered, these need to be communicated and discussed openly, so that everyone can take part in the process of finding a solution (as problems are rarely the fault of just one person or even a single team).

- Finally, at the end of the project, both sides need to sit down and review what went well and what badly, and decide what they would do differently if faced with similar problems in the future.

In summary

Transparency is one of the critical success factors in consulting projects because people who do not understand what is going on, or their role in it, can never perform well. Crucially, there has to be transparency at all levels, not just among the senior executives and their counterparts in a consulting firm. Everything depends on:

- Sending out a clear message about the project and why consultants are involved in it.

- Ensuring that this message reaches all the people involved, whatever their position or seniority.

- Being consistent during the project.

- Ensuring that transparency is maintained throughout the life of a project by being open about costs, problems and lessons learned.

Case study

CNCE

Caisse Nationale de la Caisse d'Epargne (CNCE), the national parent bank of Groupe Caisse d'Epargne, wanted to update its time and activity repository for its sales network. The project was carried out by central management control. The approach was first trialled via a pilot scheme conducted on a local Caisse d'Epargne, i.e. a dozen branches, and implemented with the ABC (Activity-Based Costing) method.

In the communication system, the CNCE management control had to be assisted by each local Caisse d'Epargne in order to share the challenges and objectives of the approach and to ensure that they were fully understood. In practice, these intermediaries were only partially effective in this role.

The need to meet and discuss with numerous players in the business elevated communication to the rank of method element: it is easy to understand why, in this respect, beyond principles and regulations, a turnkey approach was difficult to find.

In order to carry out their task and obtain the information they needed, the consultants formed a task force and, prior to holding the interviews, conducted numerous rehearsals with the client's teams who were jointly involved in the assignment. A proactive communication system was developed in the form of a communication kit. The consultants' contribution in adapting the method to the context was decisive. The quality of this preparation ensured the fluency and effectiveness of what may otherwise have been inconclusive interviews.

Once these means of communication were made available, the situational intelligence of the mixed CNCE-Logica teams ensured the analysis, sometimes at the last minute and other times intuitively, of the specific context of each interview, demonstrating the importance of systematic adaptation to the interviewee.

Prepared and contextual communication is key to the success of an assignment: it justifies taking the time needed to maintain a constant level of quality in the relationship with the client.

7

BEING INNOVATIVE; BEING FLEXIBLE

There are very few journeys that happen exactly as you plan them. Road works may block the way up ahead; an opportunity to go a few miles off route to have lunch with an old friend comes up; something you've forgotten means you have to turn back.

The same is true in consulting. However clear the idea you started with, however well-laid your plans, reality is different. Although each new problem or opportunity you encounter during the course of the project is unique, you're faced with the same three fundamental choices, ones that are no different to those you face on the road:

- You can do nothing, continuing along the same route despite the apparent obstacles.

- You can take an innovative approach, the equivalent of ditching your car to take the train.

- You can be flexible, taking a small diversion that quickly gets you back to where you wanted to be.

Doing nothing

This is rarely an option in consulting, any more than it is in travelling, but it is extraordinary how many organisations try to do it nonetheless. They may simply not know that there are alternatives (and we have all been stuck in traffic jams only to discover that, if only we'd turned off earlier, we could have circumvented the entire problem). They may be in denial, hoping that the problem will simply go away. Consulting firms can be just as guilty of this: they too, may ignore problems until they become urgent or stick too rigidly to a plan

Taking the innovative approach

There has always been a lot of talk about innovation in the consulting industry: clients are constantly hunting for it; consulting firms are always trumpeting their ability to provide it. But what does it actually mean?

Go to a consulting firm's website and you will almost inevitably encounter reports, articles, books and "white papers", all assembled under the splendidly optimistic title of "thought leadership". Indeed, the 50 largest consulting firms around the world together produce more than 5,000 pieces of thought leadership a year, although exactly how many depends on the rather thorny issue of how you define thought leadership.

Why all the attention? Quite a significant proportion of thought leadership is not designed for clients at all, but aimed at spreading ideas around the consulting firm, alerting people in different business units to the ideas of their colleagues and giving individuals the chance to promote their own personal "brand" in a big and sprawling organisation. More ambitious firms use thought leadership to keep their corporate brands in their clients' minds and establish their credentials among potential new clients. The most ambitious of all use it to try and set an agenda for an entire industry, highlighting a particular trend, then researching and analysing it over several years. The more ambitious the firm, the more money and time it puts behind its efforts.

Almost without exception, consulting firms struggle with how they market themselves. Their services are intangible and tailored to meet the needs of each client, so describing them in standardised terms devalues them. Expertise is in the heads of the consultants and resumes on a website rarely give an adequate picture. Thought leadership has therefore become one of the key marketing battlegrounds, with firms fighting over their ability to dominate particular issues.

As a client, it might be tempting to dismiss thought leadership as marketing by another name, but there are good reasons not to.

The key issue with thought leadership is not that it is all irrelevant, but that some of it is. So how can you distinguish between good and bad thought leadership? There are two things to consider here:

• Whether the subject matter is genuinely important

• The quality of the thought leadership

Does it matter?

In *The Tipping Point,* journalist Malcolm Gladwell identified three factors which would "tip" a book from being a little-known read to a bestseller, a cult film into a blockbuster or a few, isolated cases of a new disease into a pandemic:

• The power of context – when the timing with which a change emerges may be more or less helpful to its propagation

• Stickiness – the extent as to which the impact of a change is lasting

• The law of the few – where a small number of people behave in a way that, intentionally or not, increases adoption of the change.

These same factors provide a useful framework within which to consider whether the article you have just come across on the internet, or the report that has just landed unsolicited on your desk is worth paying attention to:

- The power of context: The most important pieces of thought leadership are those that tap into concerns in the wider economy and so resonate with their audience. The original thinking around business process re-engineering in United States in the early 1990s enjoyed incredibly wide adoption because it chimed with frustrations about the nature of organisations (too hierarchical) and the performance of American manufacturing businesses (unable to compete with smarter Japanese firms).

- Stickiness: Plenty of management fads come and go, attracting interest only in the short-term. The thought leadership worth giving more than a cursory glance to is that which addresses long-term, more fundamental issues: the impact of emerging economies, the implications of a new technology, new sourcing models, matching carbon management to cost management, are all examples of topics with genuine staying power because they address serious business issues.

- The law of the few: For consulting firms to invest heavily in researching a topic and developing tools or techniques to help managers deal with it, there has to be something in it for them too. A topic which is unlikely to generate more than a few days' work will not provide a good return on their investment.

The best thought leadership is therefore produced where the interests of clients and consulting firms coincide: the former can see an important issue and want ideas about how to resolve it; the latter want to respond to client needs but also have to make a profit.

Is it any good?

If a book or article engages your attention at the out-set, keeps you reading until the end and prompts you to act, then it is almost certainly good:

- **Appeal:** The "read or bin" decision is the first test of good material. If the first paragraph is sufficiently arresting to attract your attention, then, at least subliminally, you have recognised that the topic is relevant to you. Perhaps it touches on a problem you have been encountering; perhaps it relates to an opportunity you have been weighing up. Topicality is one facet here, but so too is the scale of the issue ("stickiness" as described above) and the accessibility with which it is written (a highly technical subject explained in layman's terms, for example).

- **Track-record:** It is usually the depth of research or the insights of a real expert that keep you turning the pages. Superficial research and shallow thinking, often based around just a single example, are always immediately evident. However relevant the subject-matter, you are not going to waste time reading something that is, in effect, thinly disguised marketing material.

- **Differentiation:** By the time you get to the end of the material, you want to think something new. Sometimes a book or article will have this effect because it is focused on a subject you had not considered before; sometimes it is an issue with which you are familiar, but the author has given it a distinctive and innovative twist. On a very small scale, the best thought leadership will change the way you think, just as the best consulting will change the way your organisation or people do something.

- **Commercialisation:** As we noted above, one of the ways to tell if a piece of thought leadership is going to have traction in the market as a whole is whether the consulting firm that has produced it can see a substantial commercial opportunity for itself. This will come through in the material itself: a firm that expects to earn money from its services around a specific topic will be a little keener to encourage you to act as a result of reading their material. Their research will show that a client who takes some action on the back of a piece of thought leadership is far more likely to contact, even hire, the firm than a client who simply reads the material and files it. The action itself does not matter too much – it might be forwarding it on to a colleague or picking up the phone to ask a subordinate a question the material has prompted – it is the fact that you have done something that matters. To facilitate this, some firms include questionnaires or benchmarking data: anything that will encourage you to compare your organisation's performance to that described in the article. But why should this matter to clients? Surely the "commercialisation" of thought leadership is something that matters only to the firm that writes it? Actually, it is crucial from a client point of view, too. A firm that wants to ensure you act on the basis of its thinking is more likely to have a close link between its thinking and its services: the consultants you work with will have been closely involved in producing the thought leadership and are therefore genuine experts in their field. Where a piece of thought leadership remains highly theoretical and does not encourage you to act in some way, then you might reasonably suspect it has been written by a research team, not the practicing consultants.

The stardust of consulting

However, innovation on paper is an entirely different issue than innovation in practical terms, on a consulting project. Jumping out of your car and running for the train isn't always a viable or even desirable option.

"One of the reasons I keep going back to this firm is that they know a huge amount about our industry and are willing to challenge their own – and our – assumptions. In the conventional consulting model, a partner sells the work but only turns up for occasional meetings, leaving the more junior consultants to do most of the work. However hard they work, they're working to a pattern, so you don't get any deep 'moments'. When we work with this firm, we get surprises in the best sense: they tell us things we genuinely hadn't thought of: that's stardust."

These were the words of a reasonably hard-nosed investment banker some years ago. When you ask clients what they want from a consulting firm, innovation is usually high on the agenda, although not as high as the more basic requirements such as expertise, ability to deliver and value for money. Ironically, innovation is also one of the areas where consulting firms tend to score less well in post-engagement satisfaction surveys.

When you ask clients what they want from a consulting firm, innovation and originality are usually high on the agenda, although not as high as the more basic requirements such as expertise, ability to deliver and value for money. Ironically, innovation and creativity are also two of the areas where consulting firms tend to score less well in post-engagement satisfaction surveys.

There are two reasons why this is the case:

• Clients sometimes have grandiose ideas about what they mean by innovation. The term is generally such a positive one in business that everyone always thinks it is the right thing to have (think how counterproductive it would be to say you did not want to be innovative!) But in practice people do not always need or want "innovation". If you are setting up a new call centre for a bank, you want to tap into the expertise of people who have done this for other banks, so you can avoid the first-mover disadvantage – the mistakes made and costs incurred by someone doing something for the first time. Although it may sound like heresy to admit it, the number of consulting projects that demand real, cutting-edge creativity is small: a company wants to launch a new product; a large-scale public sector organisation wants to instil innovative thinking across its middle managers; a retailer wants to find new ways to encourage its staff to offer better customer service.

• Not helped by clients who send out confusing signals about what they mean by being innovative, consulting firms do not always make this a priority. Indeed, in the majority of consulting firms, the business model is predicated on spotting new and emerging business ideas and/or technology and working out how to apply them in practice, it is not necessarily in coming up with the ideas or technology in the first place. A small number of firms are genuinely innovative, but they represent a tiny minority of the industry as a whole.

Neither of these points is intended to criticise clients nor consultants: it is entirely reasonable and in many cases economically sensible to eschew the kind of high-risk, hugely expensive activity associated with genuine innovation in favour of tried-and-tested approaches.

What is not reasonable, however, is for such ways of working to become so inflexible that they cannot be adapted to fit the unique circumstances a client firm may find itself in. The best chefs treat a recipe as a framework, a structure around which they may choose to innovate, not a rigid list that has to be followed slavishly.

That the same is true in consulting is borne out by research done by an American academic called Eric Abrahamson. Looking at the waves of management fads that washed over US businesses in the 1990s, Abrahamson concluded that the organisations that earned the greatest benefits from implementing these new ideas were those who adopted them early on. This was largely because they spent time working out how to tailor the idea to their particular needs, whereas later adopters tended to follow a set process, irrespective of their circumstances. In effect, early adopters put the end before the means; later ones focus on the means, at the expense of the end. Of course, the downside to being an early adopter, at least in management circles, is that you are taking a risk. If a new approach has not been implemented before, you are likely to encounter problems, some of which will take unscheduled time and unbudgeted money to rectify, so the greatest benefits often come with the highest costs.

As a client you want to travel somewhere between the two: staying on the same road, even when you can see problems ahead, will always invite disaster, but coming off the road, parking your car and taking the train is rarely easy. While it is helpful to understand the consulting firm's capacity to think innovatively – in effect, to explore the alternative ways of getting to your destination – what you need are practical solutions, the smart but small detours. You need new thinking – which is where a firm's thought leadership comes into play. You also need to know that this thinking has been tested in practice, but that the consultants who will work with you will use the thinking as an inspiration, not as a rigid set of rules. What innovation here actually translates into is flexibility: you need the consultants to innovate around their standard process, making it fit your needs rather than expecting you to conform to their way of working; you need them to make small adjustments not impose grand new strategies.

This takes us back to the comments of the investment banker quoted earlier. What he realised was that he wanted neither a hugely ambitious and costly level of innovation in a consulting project nor a slavish following of a pre-designed process. When he talked about innovation, what he was actually looking for was flexibility, the willingness to tailor an analytical process – to name one example – in order to generate real insight into their business and the world in which it operated.

This is the right ambition for most consulting projects. Above all else, you bring consultants in to help your organisation do something it cannot do itself. When it comes to intellectual input, you want the consultants to tell you something you did not know: as the investment banker observes, you want to be surprised.

So how can you ensure your consultants will be flexible?

• The starting point is to ask how innovative they are. As we noted above, thought leadership is not important because every client is hungry for the next big idea, but because it demonstrates the capacity of the consulting firm to think of alternatives. A firm that produces no thought leadership is unlikely to be flexible because it has limited (apparent) capacity to think laterally.

- You need to work with at least some of the consultants who are involved in producing thought leadership. It is easy for individuals to take credit for material they did not contribute to, so make sure you have some expert "map readers" on your project.

- It is important to spend time with the consultants going through their approach and debating how it needs to be tailored to your needs. This is something you should involve as many people from your side as possible in, because it is important not only to ensure that an approach really has been adjusted to fit your unique circumstances but also for the people around you to feel that they are part of the process, not that the process is being imposed upon them.

- The consultants you work with on the project need to be flexible by nature: some people are simply more bound by process, so choose your individual consultants well and change them if you think they lack the self-confidence to adapt the way they work.

- Finally, flexibility will only happen in an environment which does not reward rigid compliance. If either your organisation or the consulting firm has no tolerance for change or mistakes, or cannot handle a degree of uncertainty, then you are unlikely to find flexibility.

In summary

Every project encounters unexpected problems and opportunities which cannot be ignored. Innovative solutions are always possible on paper, but their real value lies in their capacity to help clients and consultants look at smart, but feasible, alternatives. The key on any consulting project, therefore, is not creativity per se, but flexibility: the willingness and ability of all those involved to look at alternative – and in some cases radical – solutions, but then adapt that thinking to resolve the issues faced in reality. Ensuring that this is the case depends on both the choice of the individual consultants you work with and on whether the environment, the ecosystem as we described it in Chapter 4, encourages, recognises and rewards flexibility.

Case study

DEUTSCHE TELEKOM - OPEN API CASE STUDY

Deutsche Telekom asked Logica Business Consulting to help it offer new services to its partners via a new access channel to its information system. LBC was entrusted with the task of determining the viability of this new positioning and, if it turned out to be worthwhile, of identifying ways to develop the channel. A market analysis and a benchmarking study were carried out, competitors' offerings were thoroughly scrutinised and the originality of Deutsche Telekom's target positioning was confirmed.

At that point the project entered a second phase, in which LBC worked hand-in-hand with the client's IT department to outline the functional and technical plans for this ambitious Open API project, with Deutsche Telekom retaining control over the engineering phase. In this highly innovative context, the importance of methodology was secondary, since Deutsche Telekom above all valued the contribution of ideas, sector expertise, the sharing of information and finally, rigorous project management in order to balance all of these aspects together and retain a roadmap compatible with the requirements of the sector.

This strategic project, carried out at the highest level, was communicated from the top down to every level of middle management, so as to involve all managers in the process and obtain their support and assistance in the development of this pioneering system, which is crucial to the image of Deutsche Telekom in this extremely competitive sector.

8

SHARING THE DRIVING

Carlos drummed his fingers on the table, trying to shrug off the sense of déjà vu that was settling above him like a cloud. The supply chain director from Beauty Inc's Shampoo and Soaps division was half-way through a typically lack-lustre presentation on his plans to reduce his costs by 5% – the goal that Carlos and his fellow members of the Board had set for next year's business plans. Staring at the columns of figures projected onto the screen at the other end of the meeting room, Carlos tried to identify why he was feeling uneasy. It wasn't that Don, the director, didn't know his stuff. He'd been with the company for five years, having spent the previous ten years working for a competitor organisation: he had supply chain management in his DNA. The problem, Carlos decided, was partly one of style: Don had never been a good communicator, preferring to cow his audiences into submission by doing what he was doing now – blinding them with supply chain science. This inevitably had the effect of dampening any discussion: presentations by Don were typically followed by deafening silences in which the other people round the table scrambled to come up with something intelligent to say in response. As on previous occasions, Don's business plan would be tweaked, really just for the sake of it, while everyone moved onto another area with inward sighs of relief.

But what made Don's approach doubly frustrating this year was the fact that Beauty's Skincare division had taken a different tack. This year their supply chain director had made a real effort to explain the drivers of costs within that business, the constraints under which they operated and to identify areas where significant savings could be made. For the first time in Carlos' experience, there had been a meaningful discussion about the options and what improvements could realistically be made within the timescales the Board had specified. Of course, some of the credit should go to the consultants with whom the skincare division had been working: Carlos suspected that they hadn't just helped pull together some more innovative ideas but that they'd coached the supply chain director to present them in a more engaging fashion. His only worry was whether Skincare had the experience necessary to implement the ideas being put forward.

But, turning his mind back to Shampoo and Soaps, why hadn't Don got the message? Although the consultants had primarily been working with Skincare, Don had been on the steering committee and Carlos was reasonably sure that he'd also consulted them about the plans in Shampoo and Soaps. As far as Carlos could see, he was using some of the consultants' data on industry averages, but he certainly hadn't taken their lead in terms of presentation style. Why is it, Carlos thought sourly, that consultants can have a dramatic impact on one area of a business but not on others?

Carlos' question is a good one on many levels. One of the fundamental reasons why organisations use consultants is to gain access to the latter's knowledge and skills. There are some circumstances where a client is simply looking for an expert opinion – the valuation of a potential acquisition or benchmarking the performance of an operational unit would be typical examples – but on many occasions the knowledge imparted by the consultants may have long-term value for the client. Most clients do not just want to use consultants: they want to learn from them. It is therefore frustrating, as Carlos is finding, to discover that some people do not appear to gain much from working with consultants. They read the report, even assimilate the information and use the analysis, but they do not seem to do their job any better as a result. Indeed, Carlos' experience is by no means unusual. While most clients are quick to praise the technical knowledge of consultants and recognise their ability to communicate effectively, research consistently shows that they are much less impressed by consultants' ability to share their skills. Yet, skills transfer is important because it helps individuals gain from consulting projects at a personal level (a point we will explore in greater detail in the following chapter) and because it means that the client does not become dependent on a consulting firm repeating the same piece of work. In other words, it is fundamental to success in consulting.

If you were going on a long car journey, would you expect one person to do all the driving? Of course not: you will get to your destination more quickly and more safely if you share the task. Consulting projects should never rely on one side only (the consulting firm): it is a task that needs to be shared, but it can only be shared if consultants, who after all are being used for their specialist skills, have been able to share some of those skills with people in the client organisation. You can't share the driving until you've shown the other person how to take the wheel.

Three kinds of skills

Before we look at why transferring skills from consultants to clients is apparently so difficult and what can be done to improve the process, we first need to establish what kinds of skills we are talking about.

The bedrock of consulting is **technical knowledge**. It is very hard to find a consulting assignment which does not involve an element of such knowledge: even consultants who describe themselves as generalists (strategy firms, for instance) are in practice specialists in a specific approach (strategy formulation and business modelling, for example). Technical knowledge is also the easiest type of "skill" to transfer, partly because it is visible (clients recognise what they don't know) and partly because it has been codified. A consultant's technical knowledge may come from working with a particular piece of software, from access to proprietary knowledge about a specific market, from working with academics in a specialised field, and from a host of other sources. Whatever its provenance and format, this information can be passed on to someone on the client's side relatively easily – this is precisely what Don at Beauty Inc has done.

However, consultants do not usually just bring technical skills with them, but a host of other skills that have to do with **communication, change management and stakeholder engagement** – all the skills that seem to have by-passed Don. By and large, these skills are connected to the way people work – the process, rather than the content – and, as we can see from our example at the start of this chapter, they can be just as important from a client point of view as the technical ones.

It is a point made most effectively by David Maister, whose book, *The Trusted Advisor*, has become something of a gold standard for professional firms. Maister's formula for creating trust depends on three factors: credibility, reliability and intimacy. He makes the point that credibility relates primarily to the technical knowledge of an advisor and shows itself in the advisor's words (what he or she tells to the clients). Reliability, according to Maister's model, comes from the actions people take, when they say – for example – they are going to finish a piece of work by a given date and actually do so. The third and final component of trust Maister termed "intimacy", picking up on the idea that it was a host of softer skills which have as much to do with the consultant's personality as with their experience. Without intimacy, an advisor can come across as a simple technician, capable of analysing the data without really engaging with the issue or people in hand. It is precisely these kinds of skills that Don has not picked up, although clearly his colleague has done so. As this suggests, such skills are harder to transfer than technical knowledge: they are less codified and are much more dependent on an individual's personality.

The third and final "skill" consultants bring is **experience**, the ability to draw on a wide range of previous work and draw from it the practical and relevant lessons they have learned. This is clearly the hardest skill to transfer because it is only acquired over considerable time. Both Don and his counterpart in Beauty Inc's Skincare division have considerable expertise, although perhaps acquired from only a limited number of other organisations, but Carlos is right to be concerned that they may lack direct experience of some of the more radical ideas being proposed.

Overcoming the barriers to sharing skills

Organisations like Beauty Inc face four fundamental problems in trying to learn from the consultants they use:

1. **Lack of time and investment:** Skills transfer may be something that is high on most clients' agenda when it comes to using consultants but it is not always an issue to which they give much serious consideration. As budgets get spent and timescales are eaten into, clients will focus more and more on the deliverables, often at the expense of the process. Many clients I have met over the years complained that they set up projects in such a way to ensure the transfer of skills from consultant to client only to find that, as the final deadline approached, any attempt to do so was abandoned in the effort to reach a successful conclusion. "Skills transfer often becomes a nice-to-have during the course of the project," was how one client put it, "which of course means we never get to have it."

2. **Fear among consultants of cannibalising their services:** Given that consultants' core business is taking knowledge and

ideas from one organisation to another, consulting firms might understandably be reluctant to train their clients too effectively and lose revenue as a result. This is a widespread suspicion among clients and one that consulting firms have done little to counter. In fact, the barriers here are far more likely to be logistical than conspiratorial. Working to tight budgets, consultants are also likely to treat skills transfer as an optional extra, to be sacrificed in order to meet tangible and commercially crucial deadlines.

3. **An absence of techniques to share skills:** Both sides are equally guilty of not putting enough thought into what is actually meant by skills transfer or how it is to be achieved. Instead they often assume that the process will occur as if by osmosis. "If we bring such-and-such a consulting firm in," client thinking goes, "then we're bound to learn something from them." Similarly, the consultants tend to think: "If we use so-and-so on this piece of work, he's bound to be able to take the client's people along with him."

4. **Organisational complexity:** The ability of consultants to share their skills with clients is in direct proportion to the extent they work alongside them. Consulting projects are like stones thrown into a pond: their impact ripples out in a series of concentric and increasingly weak rings from a central point. Unsurprisingly, if you quiz the people involved from a client's side, you tend to find that those who work most closely with consultants (the supply chain director from Beauty Inc's Skincare division) absorb more of the latter's skills than those who have less to do with the consultants (Don).

From this, it is clear that the first critical success factor in ensuring that, if skills transfer is something the client genuinely wants to achieve as opposed to simply pay lip-service to, then it needs to be a concrete part of the work the consultants are contracted to do, not assumed to be part of the way they work. This does not mean you have to lay out in considerable details what skills you would like which members of your team to acquire, but that you make an allowance in the project plan and budget for this activity to take place. It needs to be ring-fenced in some way as well, to ensure that neither side is tempted to re-use the money to plug shortfalls in other activities.

The second factor is to consider how best to transfer each of the three types of skills outlined above, not only to the immediate project team (which is comparatively easy) but to other areas of your organisation (something that is much harder to achieve). Figure 2 provides a framework for doing this and highlights five key activities which together would go a long way to improving the level of skills transfer taking place in consulting projects.

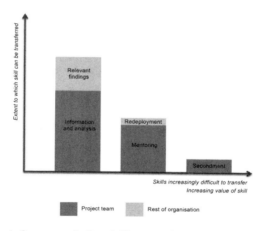

Figure 2: A framework for skills transfer in consulting projects

- **Technical knowledge:** The key here is **information and analysis**. You need a commitment from the consulting firm to pass over as much of the material it has gathered and other sources to those directly involved in the project. You also want to ensure that your people have the opportunity to work with the consultants gathering the data, whether that means taking part in internal meetings, going to other organisations when possible, or attending external training courses alongside the consultants. Spreading this knowledge beyond the immediate team is inevitably more of a challenge because people are generally only interested in what is immediately relevant to them in their jobs and given that some types of technical knowledge are very specific, most feel that not everyone needs to be an expert in everything. Absorbing information and analysis requires time and commitment and you cannot expect people whose jobs do not depend on it to pay anything much more than cursory attention to it. It is therefore critical to extract from the immediate consulting project the **relevant findings** which are applicable to other parts of the organisation and disseminate these messages alongside the conclusions of the project.

- **"Intimacy skills"**: As these have more to do with behaviour than intellectual frameworks, the most effective ways of transferring them from consultant to client is to ensure that the two work simply together during the course of the project and that the consultants have the responsibility for **mentoring** their counterparts, identifying the softer skills which will help them develop the latter's careers and build their capabilities as managers. The key to passing on such skills more widely within an organisation is to try and replicate this mode of learning as far as possible, by the **re-deployment** of people who have worked on the consulting project elsewhere, into positions in which their newly-acquired management skills can be used, demonstrated and passed on to the teams who work for them. As with all areas of skills transfer, this will not happen by accident, but needs to be planned and executed carefully.

- **Experience**: The wealth of experience consultants should bring to a project is the hardest of all "skills" to transfer simply because it is based on something (exposure to the successes and failures of past projects) that is hard to compress into the timescales of a single project. To a degree, the technical knowledge that the consultant brings, combined with the "intimacy" skills acquired during those past projects, encapsulates some of the consultant's experience but it is almost impossible to distil all of it. What remains is the consultant's *practical* experience.

What may help here is to negotiate opportunities in which people from the client side are **secondments** to the consulting firm, to work with them for a period of time or on a specific project for another organisation. Clearly, this cannot be done *en masse*: there is no obvious way of transferring the experience of consultants more widely within an organisation.

This last point is crucial. It sounds negative: this is something that clients and consultants cannot do. In fact, it suggests why consulting as an activity continues to exist and why consultants should not, therefore, be concerned that skills transfer will in anyway cannibalise their future revenue. It is precisely because it takes a long time to acquire such experience and because it is consequently very difficult to pass it on to others, that organisations go back to expert consultants time and time again.

In summary

Sharing skills is critical to any successful consulting project. Without it, clients become too dependent on the consulting firm and people within the client's organisation become disaffected. However, it is by no means a straight-forward process and it is dangerous to assume that skills can be transferred by some form of accidental osmosis. Effective sharing of skills requires thought and planning. It also involves recognising that consultants bring different types of skills, some of which are more easily shared than others:

- Technical knowledge, usually in the form of data and analysis, is the simplest to share, providing that the consulting firm is committed to doing so and that relevant findings only are disseminated.

- "Intimacy skills", the softer skills which consultants are so often valued for, can only be passed on from individual to individual, via a systematic mentoring process. Time and money has to be put aside in any project budget for this to be achieved.

Practical experience accumulated by the consultants from the previous projects they have worked on is impossible to share in a conventional sense. The most effective way of doing this is to second people from the client organisation to work in the consulting firm so they can gain the experience themselves from first-hand exposure to other organisations.

One of the world's largest retailers

The company concerned with this case study has patiently grown over the past forty years to become one of the world's largest retailers. It has over 12 500 stores, more than 400 000 employees and is present in 30 countries. In order to gain performance and rationalize costs, it has launched a global project of developing a unique information system for all the negotiation processes: from purchasing data consolidation to negotiations management and billing follow-up.

The platform had to be implemented in 21 countries. Three waves were phased: first a pilot deployment in three countries (Turkey, Brazil and Poland), thirteen new countries the year after for the second wave, and then the five last countries. The main challenges were to define the best practices and implement a global and standardized model, in order to build this unique Information System solution.

Our consultants defined a deployment kit covering all the deployment needs, starting with the communication management, the IT and business changes, the organizational impacts, the training plan......

They designed the strategy and the communication plan, and then coordinated communication activities and implementation with project newsletters and presentation to sponsors. They also designed and supervised the whole training which was strategic and critical for the project: training plan, train the internal trainers, training kits, users guidebooks. Finally, they analyzed impacts on users (organizational, cultural, jobs, processes) and set up guidance actions.

1 500 users were trained and skilled to face business change, and the bottom line showed best practices standardized within the 21 countries of the group.

9

ENGAGING EVERYONE ENTHUSIASM

It is a truism of business that no employee gets out of bed on a Monday morning motivated by the desire to improve their organisation's share price. People are motivated by many things: the performance of a business is rarely the most important one.

When you work with or alongside management consultants, one of the things that will strike you is that most of them (there are always exceptions) want to do the best possible job for their clients. Satisfied clients are easier and more pleasant to work with; a successful project gives a sense of a job well done; there is pride in being able to come in and fix things; good work will ultimately translate into promotion, greater rewards within the consulting firm and perhaps even greater recognition outside of it. Indeed, consultants often feel more loyalty to their clients than they do to their employers: look how many of them leave to join clients as employees or at how little attention consultants generally pay to running their own firms. Generally, they would rather spend time with their clients (where they can get things done) than on internal politics (where they are subject to the same barriers and frustration any employee feels). Consultants therefore do get out of bed on Monday mornings, wanting to make sure that a project succeeds.

The executive who sponsors a consulting project is, of course, also motivated to ensure it succeeds. Having signed off what may be a considerable amount of money for a project, his or her career will undoubtedly be blighted if the project is seen to fail. But people working lower down the organisational hierarchy may think differently:

- Even before the consultants have arrived, they feel disengaged, perhaps because there has been tremendous amounts of upheaval as a result of a merger or acquisition, or because they feel their job might be threatened by cost-cutting, or because they find their work boring and perceive their careers to be stalled or even blocked. Unlike consultants, "ordinary" employees cannot get out of the office completely or side-step internal politics.

- The advent of consultants may trigger a greater feeling of dissatisfaction. As we have already noted in earlier chapters, employees can feel marginalised, believing that their senior managers would prefer to listen to consultants rather than colleagues. Poor preparation may well mean that they feel uninformed and mistrustful.

In such circumstances, it is unsurprising that the successful conclusion of a consulting project may not seem to be their top priority. All this matters because the potential cost of employees not being motivated to help a project succeed can be enormous. Often, it is the discretionary effort of employees – the extra mile that people inevitably have to go during the course of a project, however good the planning may be – is the difference between success and failure. Clients worry about consulting project over-runs for example. They suspect that this is the consulting firms' fault, by not scoping the work out correctly in the first place or by trying to sell in additional services either during or after the project. While there is an element of truth to this, research suggests that, more often than not, it is the end-user who is at fault. It is the end-users, not the consultants, who are most likely to be confused about the scope of a project. They are also likely to promise more than they deliver: information required by the consultants is often delivered late; meetings are delayed because it proves almost impossible to get the multiple stakeholders involved together in a room. All of this does not only cost time but also money: delays during the project almost inevitably mean that the consultants have to do more work than planned and the overall bill for the project rises.

By contrast, I have been struck by a common theme that emerges when you talk to people who have been involved, from the client's side, in successful consulting projects. Here's how one organisation put it:

> "We've seen a number of projects which were all consulting-led. They were effectively ignored by people here and there was absolutely no buy-in to the final result. Having joint teams is the starting point, but that's only a means to an end – giving our people a chance to think differently about something, the opportunity to stand back from their day-to-day work and engage in more challenging thinking.... The real value in using consultants lies in transferring knowledge to us, so that we can become our own experts. The best consulting projects help people develop at a personal level."

Joint working and not imposing a rigid methodology are both important to people who work side by side with consultants, but the single most important factor in making the relationship work at this very personal level is the extent to which the people involved from the client side stand to gain something from the experience. After all, why should they put up with the disruption of having consultants in if they don't benefit?

Consulting projects can – and should – open up new career opportunities for those involved, as these comments, also from clients, demonstrate:

- "We've learned a lot about process design from working alongside the consultants, and we're doing most of the follow-up work ourselves. That has created new possibilities for the people involved as we roll out the work in different parts of the business."

- "We're really proud about what we've achieved here and we're actively encouraging those involved to take on more responsibilities both here and in other areas."

- "The work we did energised our business at all levels. We found people, some of whom had downshifted, others had got stuck in dusty corners of our business, but all of them were bright enough to see the potential for doing interesting work – and involved them in the programme. For these people, the project has been a springboard to new, better careers."

Variations on a theme

As these comments indicate, ensuring that individuals – as well as organisations – gain from the presence of consultants can take many different forms, the most important of which are highlighted in the table below, starting with the "gains" that require least effort and co-ordination and moving on to those that need most. Common across all of them, however, is the need to ensure that this facet of the client-consultant relationship is actively planned into projects: don't assume it will happen by accident:

Figure 3: Ensuring everyone gains from a consulting project

Individual gain	What is involved?	What type of pre-planning is required?
Internal recognition	• The key here is for someone to see that their input is praised and their role on the project is acknowledged by other colleagues.	• Both client and consulting team need to ensure that the person has the opportunity to present the findings of the project, or a summary of its achievements, to their immediate colleagues. • It is also helpful to consider coverage of the project team and their achievements in internal magazines and newsletters.
Re-starting a career that has slowed	• Picking someone out from relative obscurity and asking them to make an important contribution to a project.	• This is an all-or-nothing approach: inviting someone who has missed out on past promotions to play a peripheral role in a project may only compound their sense of being marginalised. Instead, they need, to be given a role that is integral to the project, one that appeals to their strengths while also giving them new avenues to explore. Doing this successfully requires careful thought and review of a project's organisational chart. • It also involves resisting the temptation (and many organisations fall into this trap) to put consultants into the more important full-time roles, because it is much harder to free up internal people. Before jumping to the conclusion that this is the right way forward, time should be spent looking to see exactly what resources are available internally.

Opportunity to build a reputation and network within the organisation	• Giving someone a role that involves liaising with senior executives.	• Again, achieving this depends on having a close look at the roles and responsibilities within the project hierarchy in order to identify positions that will maximise the opportunity people have to network internally. • However, access is one thing, but forging relationships with senior people is something else altogether. It is therefore particularly important to build some mentoring into the project (a point discussed in more detail below).
Direct opportunities for promotion	• Ensuring that a person has a new (and better) position to move onto, once the project is finished.	• Although it is sometimes possible for a person involved in a successful project to move onto a completely different role in an organisation, it is more likely that they either step into the shoes of the consultants when the latter leave, or move across to a different part of an organisation to carry out a similar project, but this time in the capacity of an internal consultant. This approach has benefits all round: the individual gains a new, more challenging role, while the organisation ensures a seamless transition from the consulting team to the internal team. • Thus, for this to work successfully, thought has to be given during the project to its handover and what will happen post-implementation. Again, the temptation to keep the consultants on for longer should be resisted.

It can be attractive, especially where the consultants are being hired to work on a high-profile, critically important project, to ensure that only senior, highly thought-of people are involved. This works so far as those people believe that they too, will gain something from a successful conclusion, but quite often it is other staff, whose skills are underused, who will bring the most commitment. As a result, another aspect common to all these approaches is that they require trust – trust that the people who are being asked to help will perform well in practice. Of course, there are incentives to doing so, as we have already discussed, but there are also actions the client and consulting firm can do to help ensure this happens:

- **A clear "contract":** People need to gain something from the project in practice, not in theory, so it is important to set out exactly what you expect from the individuals involved and what you undertake to provide them. Sometimes this means being quite unsubtle ("This project will give you an excellent opportunity to meet senior managers across the world and develop your network....") but better that than ambiguity. There is nothing so soul-destroying as uncertainty.

- **Part of the team:** Whether you have brought in someone who has been sitting in a career backwater for a number of years or a bright, but new, recruit, confidence will play a crucial role. The best way to engender this is to ensure that the person is very much a part of the project team: just because they may feel peripheral to the wider organisation, does not mean that they have to feel the same within the project.

- **Constant feedback:** Confidence will also grow when people are getting immediate feedback about their performance and suggestions for improvement. Someone on the project team, ideally from the consulting side, who will have no preconceptions about the individual involved, should be ear-marked to provide this feedback and time for doing so needs to be built into the project timetable. If this does not happen, the demands of the project (a budget and deadline to meet) will crowd out these activities, destroying rather than building the confidence of those involved.

- **Mentoring:** More than providing simple feedback, consultants can play a hugely important role in coaching people and helping them fulfil more of their potential. There are relatively few people within an organisation who are able or willing to provide objective and disinterested feedback, but consultants can. Moreover, the softer skills and broader range of experience that consultants bring often give them a better perspective when it comes to possible improvements.

One final point – and this is true for all aspects of a consulting project, not just the way in which internal staff can gain from them – it is important to ensure that, once the consultants finish their project and leave, neither the organisation as a whole nor the individuals working within it do not revert back to the way they were before the consultants arrived. The whole point – you could argue, the only point – of using consultants is to help an organisation do something that it could not do for itself. This applies to individuals too. The only way that they will genuinely believe that consultants have added value is if they have been changed in some way for the better. If the project finishes and the manager whose career had stalled simply returns to their old job, or the raw recruit has not been able to make an impact, or the persons expecting promotion find themselves still sitting in their old position, then the project cannot truly be said to have succeeded.

In summary

Very few organisations or consulting firms give thought as to the motivation of the people from the client side who work alongside them. Clients tend to assume that they will simply do as they are told; consulting firms assume that they are just as committed to success as the consultants are. Neither assumption is automatically correct. Moreover, there is a huge difference between the "standard" amount of effort people are prepared to put in and their willingness to put in the extraordinary effort needed for even the best-planned project to succeed. Harnessing the latter enthusiasm depends on ensuring that everyone, irrespective of their role and seniority on the consulting project, gains from the experience. Such gains can take many forms, from promotion to greater job satisfaction, from the opportunity to meet senior people to a chance to acquire new skills – but they call require thought and preparation. Like so much else in consulting, this cannot be left to chance.

Case study

NATIXIS

Two French insurance companies, MMA and MAAF, were launching a range of retail banking services on the French market. They benefited from a partnership with Natixis Retail Banking, which supplied them with banking desktops and associated back-office tools.

In addition to requiring specialist expertise, the companies had insufficient human resources to cover demand and therefore began the search for a consulting partner. Several consulting firms responded to the call, including Logica Business Consulting, which played a decisive role in ensuring effective co-operation between all of the parties.

In order to achieve this aim, individual and collective benefits were put into perspective, thereby guaranteeing the establishment of a friendly working atmosphere and a fully cohesive project team.

Subsequently the entire team, which was totally mixed and composed of both internal and external contributors, was empowered with significant responsibility and liaised directly with the business teams, which is traditionally a source of motivation for consultants.

Above all, the constant commitment of each participant stemmed from the knowledge that they were involved in a unique and functionally rich project, relating to the launch of a new range of banking services in a market targeted by the bancassurance project sponsor, based on a relatively new partnership linked to new technologies.

The project itself was visible externally and announced in the press, maximising the pride of those involved in it and enriching the resumes of the participating consultants.

Shared challenges, an ambitious and innovative project, and joint teams: individual performance was put to collective use to ensure that the final success belonged to everyone.

10
TRAVELLING TOGETHER

Philip Burnford joined the consulting industry in 1964 when he was offered a job with MSL, the firm that dominated the market in management recruitment. Many of his clients were medium-sized manufacturing companies. "Often they were pretty cosy places," he recalls. "People were promoted simply because they were next in line. They had no training for management, and no real understanding of what it required. They were very set in their ways and suspicious of anyone from outside the company, particularly of anyone better qualified than they were." He remembers visiting a well-known manufacturer of agricultural machinery: "I was talking to the black-suited company secretary, who was fairly typical of the time and who doubled as a quasi staff manager. We had agreed the specification for the development engineers they urgently needed when we were interrupted by the shuffling entrance of a very old gentleman, with a resplendent watch chain. It was the chairman and founder of the company. He listened for a while and then said: 'Don't go sending us any of those graduates. You can't learn engineering at university.' The company survived about another ten years."

"MSL was quite establishment," Burnford recalls, "with secretaries from the most expensive schools; many of the thirty or so consultants came from the armed services or were retired diplomats." MSL charged a fee of 15 percent of the job salary, most of which was paid upfront, regardless of the outcome; most work came through referrals or repeat business but 80 percent of sales visits resulted in an assignment. Burnford was 29 when he joined the consultancy; the average age of his colleagues was well over fifty. "I was paid ££3,000 a year and that was a lot of money," he remembers.

Consulting isn't what it used to be

For decades around the time that Burnford joined the consulting industry, the archetypal consultant was a man in his fifties, wearing a conservative, grey suit, wielding a substantial briefcase. As waves of American consulting firms expanded across the Western world, this popular image was supplanted by another: the brash young man from business school with a sharp brain and even sharper suit. Although conjuring up very different pictures, these two stereotypes share one common theme – the "otherness" of consultants.

"Otherness" is not necessarily bad: indeed, around half of all consulting is bought because the consultants bring specialist skills and experience which is not available in the client organisation, so in this sense "otherness" is core to what consultants do and is a key way in which they differentiate themselves from their clients. But "otherness" does have a darker side: all too often it can evolve into arrogance as consultants, keen to maintain what they perceive to be their intellectual advantage, see themselves as better than their clients. "Otherness" creates barriers too: we all find it hard to get on with people who rely on technical jargon or whose backgrounds and attitudes are very different to our own. In these circumstances, "otherness" creates resentment and distrust.

This results in a huge problem for consultants: they find themselves trapped between the Scylla and Charybdis of consulting projects. Research suggests that clients who are involved in projects where the aim of using consultants was to bring in knowledge or specialist skills not available internally are twice as likely to be satisfied as those involved in other projects where the motivation for using consultants was quite different. However, such projects, if not managed carefully, are also more likely to make the people in the client organisation feel resentful because they will not feel part of the process. The best example of this is when the consulting team, having gathered all the information it needs, perhaps as the basis of a new corporate strategy, returns to its own offices to discuss and analyse the data. The clients left behind feel resentful on many levels: they may suspect the consultants are talking about them behind their backs; they may think the consultants have the interesting work (the analysis) while they are left with the more boring aspects (gathering data); they may feel excluded as important decisions are made. Above all else, they probably feel that the consultants do not think they are good enough to be involved in the process: why else would the consultants go back to their own office? Of course, from the consultants' point of view, returning to base will make perfect sense: it will be more convenient, save the client money and mean they are in a familiar setting where they are probably more productive.

If we look at instances where consultants are brought in for other reasons, perhaps to ensure that a large and complex project is successfully delivered or to provide an outside, more objective perspective, client satisfaction rates tend to be lower, especially among junior staff. As we have discussed in early chapters, this has as much to do with lack of communication and confused messages within the client organisation as it has do with the consultants themselves. But it is also a sign that the consultants typically working on such projects tend to be less expert: they may have broad experience across many areas and their skill lies in integrating the skills of others, but they are not technical specialists to the same extent. Such consultants look less different: a consultant who comes in to facilitate a difficult discussion about the future strategy of an organisation, for example, will be skilled in getting people to contribute to a debate, a skill which, at best, is invisible to those involved. They will participate without feeling "facilitated". The problem is that, when they go back over the debate in their minds, they may question what exactly the consultant did. Here, the lack of "otherness" is a problem: because the consultant looks so much like the client's staff, some of those staff will not understand why the consultant is there. However, offset against this issue is the fact that, because the consultant looks and behaves in a way that is similar to the people on the client side, he or she is less immediately alienating.

Figure 4 illustrates this situation in diagrammatic terms. The consultants working on the corporate strategy are respected by clients because they are bringing specific expertise, but they are simultaneously resented by them because they work by themselves. Conversely, the consultant who facilitates the difficult debate is easier for people to get on with – he seems more like one of them – but the client's staff does not see that he is bringing any particular skill which would justify his fee. In other words, expertise and the ability to work seamlessly with a client are often mutually exclusive. To make effective use of consultants, you have to square this particular circle. You have to ensure that consultants, however good their technical expertise is, are also prepared to overcome the "otherness" that is inherent in the consulting process and, to some extent, often part of their outlook and behaviour.

What's the key lesson? If you're going on a journey, you need a travelling companion.

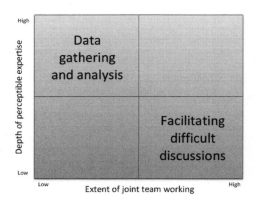

Figure 4: Expertise versus joint team working

Getting people to work together

Almost every consulting firm talks of "working in partnership with its clients". Indeed, the sentiment is so widespread that you would be hard-pushed to find a firm that did not make some reference to this in its marketing material or values. But finding out what is meant by such statements is usually much more difficult. For some firms, it appears to mean little more than "we will not be actively rude to our clients", while others clearly take the idea more seriously.

To put flesh on these bones, it is helpful to think of "travelling together" in two ways (and you could argue that successful collaboration are always a combination of the two). At a corporate level, the aims of each side (client and consultant) need to be closely matched. Each party needs an incentive to behave and contribute in a way which supports the collective effort, not self-interest. Chapter 3 (Shaping the ecosystem) and chapter 4 (Building commitment to the journey) have already covered many aspects of this, so we will focus here on the second dimension: at an individual level, people simply have to get along. A close working relationship, mutual respect and openness among the people involved will carry a project through the bad times as well as the good far more effectively than a contract will.

So how do you get your staff to work with your consultants, and vice versa? Seven key steps emerge:

1. **Establish a clear set of rules:** First, you need to make it absolutely clear to the consulting firm you are working with that this is what you want to do. Clients are just as prone as consultants to wax lyrical about the benefits of collaborative working while remaining vague about the practical details. Your intention needs to be completely clear to the consulting firm from the outset and you need to establish what is, and what is not, acceptable.

2. **Clarify division of responsibility:** Although collaborative working brings many advantages, it also involves some risks. Most significant among these is the danger that overlapping roles, performed by people from different organisations who do not yet know each other well, can result in problems going unnoticed or being missed, or in responsibility being shunted from one group of people to another. It is therefore doubly important to ensure that everyone is clear about their role and contribution and that they are collaborating, not competing.

3. **Ensure physical proximity:** It is extremely difficult for a group of people, especially if they come from diverse backgrounds to get together as a team if they are not based in the same office. Most of us will have worked in very effective teams who are distributed in different locations, even different time zones, people whom we usually email or call but rarely see face-to-face. However, most of these teams grew out of some point at which everyone was physically together, even if only briefly. In practical terms, this means you should find space for your consultants to work in your offices, ideally next to the people with whom they will be working. And "space" here has to be decent and reasonable: one retired consultant recalled being sent out to a manufacturing company which made its resentment at his presence felt by putting him in a tiny glass office with one small steel desk and chair where everyone could watch him. Not surprisingly, he took every opportunity to go back to his own office.

4. **Invest time and money understanding difference:** There are a wide variety of tools you can now use to help team members appreciate their varied strengths and weaknesses. Myers Briggs$^{(TM)}$ and Belbin$^{(TM)}$, are two of the more obvious ones that spring to mind: they both make the point that people with different preferences may well find each other hard to work with but that teams require a combination. To use Belbin's classification just as an illustration, a team needs a

"chairman" to co-ordinate its activity; it has to have "plants" and "shapers" to come up with ideas and challenge them; and it must have "completer finishers" to ensure the good ideas come to fruition. Both clients and consultants use such techniques internally, with their own teams, but they tend to assume that they do not need to do so where there is a joint client-consultant team. Perhaps each side assumes the other has it in hand; perhaps they assume that the consultants, if they are professional, can be relied on to get on with everyone. Whatever the cause, the net effect is that this stage is often forgotten – at least until it is too late.

5. **Have a crisis:** There is no more effective (or efficient) way of discovering how well you work with other people than by working into the early hours of the morning producing a crucial document or meeting a critical deadline. Working in such circumstances tells us who we can rely on, who can crack a joke while under pressure, and indeed who fails to make the grade. You might want to test out how effective your joint team will be before the project starts, perhaps even before you have selected the consulting firm you want to work with, by getting people together for a workshop or event designed to highlight team chemistry. Alternatively, or in addition, you might want to ensure there is an early milestone in the project which will force people to work in a very concentrated fashion.

6. **Agree common standards:** Nothing reinforces "otherness" more than two sets of rules, one for the client people and one for the consultants, even on the same project. This can be as trivial as dress code or working hours, both issues which are easily fixed, but can touch on more fundamental concerns (the difference in pay, for example) which are much harder to resolve. However, the detail matters less than the intent: it is important for people on the client side to see that the consultants are not privileged and for the consultants to have no excuse for arrogance. Although it is helpful to discuss and

resolve such issues up front, the willingness to be treated equitably is also a cultural issue, something some consulting firms (and some consultants) feel more comfortable with than others.

7. **Switch people around:** However hard you try to prevent it, there will always be some people who do not get on or who do not sit comfortably with the rest of the team. In such situations, the only real solution is to replace them with someone else. Often clients do not think about this with internal projects because, as everyone is always so busy with their day jobs, it can be difficult to find enough people for a given team in the first place, let alone swap people in and out where they do not fit. Thus, participants in internal teams often accept that they have no choice and accept poor performance or lack of participation from their colleagues. Consulting firms may be similarly constrained (all their consultants may be busy on other assignments), but their business model is designed to be able to move people around, often at quite short notice, and this is one of the reasons why clients use consultants rather than rely wholly on internal teams. It is therefore not unreasonable to expect the consulting firm to change their people if the need arises. However, the crucial aspect of making this work is to ensure, first, that you have regular (timetabled) discussions with the project manager and/or the overall director of the assignment at which you discuss how well individuals are working, and second, that you accept and act on, wherever possible, feedback from the consultants about the calibre of your own staff.

All of these steps are important: if the balance of skills and contribution is skewed, the team will never be really a "joint" one, it will always have a tendency to shift towards the side which is adding most value.

In summary

Collaboration is not just something that happens between organisations (as we discussed in Chapter 4), but between individuals. However, collaborating on a consulting project is not simple. Typically the client-consultant relationship falls into one of two categories: one in which either a deep level of technical expertise is required from the consultants which makes it difficult for the two sides to work together, or one where the consultant is playing the role of a facilitator and develops almost too close a relationship with the client. Genuine collaboration depends on:

• Clarity – of rules, roles and standards common to all those involved

• Closeness – working literally side by side with each other

• Cost – collaboration does not happen by accident nor for free

• Crisis – testing people's mettle in an emergency

• Change – switching people around when necessary

Case study

CNCE

Within the framework of the project presented in the case study for chapter 5 (updating of the time and activity repository of Caisse Nationale de la Caisse d'Epargne), Logica and CNCE worked together to form a joint team in which no distinction was made between internal and external personnel. This team stayed together throughout the duration of the programme and ensured the continuous transfer of information.

In fact, contrary to certain received ideas, judiciously shared information can unlock numerous doors. This immersion principle thus guaranteed the synchronisation of information and the fluency of exchanges between the interviewees on the one hand and the dedicated programme teams on the other.

Benefiting from the first-hand contextual knowledge brought to the table by internal staff, the consultants were able to gain a better understanding of the issues to be dealt with. They also prepared the ground with experts whose experience was recognised by their peers, reducing the risk of poor-quality interviews or even interviewees frustrated by their content. The synergy between the contextual knowledge of the internal personnel and the perspective and vision of the external consultants was apparent to all.

Far from being mere providers of expertise, the consultants were invited to express their opinion as regards coaching and the management of the project, which generally speaking is often not the case when joint teams are involved. This unequivocal openness on the part of CNCE was considered one of the key factors in the success of the operation.

Part 4

TRAVELLING ABROAD

11

MANAGING INTERNATIONAL
PROJECTS

Just to set your expectations: this is not a chapter about international relations in business as a whole. Much has been written on this subject, often with considerable sensitivity and insight. Moreover, subsequent chapters of this book will look in detail at how the client-consultant relationship varies in specific countries.

Instead, this chapter focuses on international consulting projects: how the challenges posed by having outsiders involved in your organisation can be multiplied when they are working across borders and how best to resolve the issues that will, almost inevitably, arise. Its aim is to provide an overall framework for thinking about cross-border projects and the foundation for the more in-depth discussions in the next section.

Classifying international consulting projects

Let's start by understanding what we mean by an international consulting project. That's simple, I hear you say, it is just a project that involves people from different countries. In practice, this straight-forward definition is complicated by two factors: the people involved and the overall approach adopted throughout the project, as Figure 5 illustrates.

- **Type 1 projects** are the least complicated. Although working across borders, both client and consulting teams are made up of people from one country or similar cultures and/or speaking the same language (people from the US and the UK, for example). The key here is homogeneity: this is a group of people who, because of their back-grounds, is capable of acting in unison. Poten-tial cultural and linguistic barriers are negligible and certainly not suffi-cient to have any material impact on the smooth-running of the project.

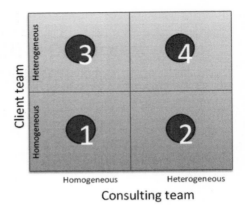

Figure 5: Classifying international consulting

- In **Type 2 projects**, the client team continues to be drawn from the same or similar countries and cultures, but the consulting team is now populated with people from a much more hetero-geneous background. Perhaps the consulting firm needs to pull in highly specialised resources from a particular country where it has a centre of excellence. Perhaps the composition of the consulting team has been deliberately designed to ensure that the client gets access to different perspectives – introducing consultants from a specific country into which the client wants to expand, but about which its people know very little, would be a good example.

- **Type 3 projects** are the mirror image of this, involving a range of people from different countries and cultures on the client side, but consultants from just one (or very similar) country and/or culture. Tensions here are both more obvious and more serious. There is a danger that the consultants, because they bring a single culture, and probably a single-minded approach, fail to recognise or take into account the cultural sensitivities of the people they are working with. They might, for example, simplify a set of HR processes across – say – a pan-European company without giving sufficient thought to the extent to which the role of the HR team may vary from country to country. Widespread resentment may result and, even if people in the different countries do adopt the changes, they are more likely to fall back on their old practices as time passes. However, as we shall see below, this tension can sometimes be both creative and valuable.

- In **Type 4 projects** the opportunities for problems multiply. Here, both the client and consulting teams are drawn from different parts of the world, so the potential for misunderstanding is rife. However, the bigger threat comes from different approaches and perceptions, making it hard to agree on a single way forward. In this scenario, a project to implement new HR processes and systems is likely to become swamped by the level of variety accepted. Each country team will include its own requirements and the sense of being part of a common venture will be limited.

Classifying projects in this way inevitably highlights the problems that accompany them. However, it would be wrong to assume that Type 3 projects are in some way "worse" than Type 2 projects, and that Type 4 projects are to be avoided at all costs. The key to success here, as in so much consulting, lies in understanding what is appropriate to a given set of circumstances.

It should also be noted that throughout this chapter we try to emphasise that homogeneity and heterogeneity are not simply a function of nationality but also of culture. Thus it is possible for a group of people from different countries to be culturally homogeneous. Indeed, some multinational companies and consulting firms make a virtue of the fact that their culture is consistent across all geographies, languages and nationalities.

Adapting your approach to the needs of the project

There are certain circumstances in which homogeneity is essential, but others where it is not simply irrelevant but even a potential barrier to success. Similarly, heterogeneity may be the death of some projects but breathe life into others.

Broadly speaking, homogeneous projects are about standardisation and compliance. If, for instance, you want to spread a new network management system across a range of nationwide offices, the key will be to ensure that exactly the same package is implemented with an identical set of parameters in all countries. The most efficient and effective way to do this is to install it in one country first, then to use the team involved in the original project to roll-out the software elsewhere. They know exactly how to set up the new system and they are best placed to replicate this elsewhere; by contrast, relying on independent teams in different countries is likely to lead to misunderstandings, mistakes and customisation. Another example especially pertinent in the current environment is regulation. A financial services company will have stringent standards for handling data security; its reputation and even viability as a company will depend on these being followed to the letter. Again, it would make sense to use a team from one country, who have established and tested the standard, ironing out any problems in the process, to move from country to country repeating their work. In both these cases, the underlying objective is to set a single standard and make sure there is no deviation from it.

Again speaking equally broadly, heterogeneous projects are concerned with people: employees and customers. A project that seeks to increase employee engagement across several countries will founder if it is staffed by people (from the client or consulting side) who come from one country and do not appreciate the nuances in employee relations elsewhere. Similarly, it is impossible to develop an effective marketing strategy for a new product to be launched in several countries which does not take into account the differences in local markets – as many multinational consumer products companies have found out to their cost. It is here that Type 4 projects come into their own: rather than trying to adopt a single approach, each country or market will have one that is tailored to its unique circumstances. In this case, success comes from recognising and building on the differences, not erasing them.

However, between these two extremes – the homogeneous and heterogeneous projects – are those that combine an element of each, and it is these that pose more problems from a project management point of view. The example given above, of the new HR processes and systems, is typical. Assuming that the overarching aim of the project is to ensure that the entire organisation follows a single approach, perhaps in order to drive down the costs of HR administration and even pave the way for a shared services centre or outsourcing contract, the challenge is to ensure that the demands of different countries do not complicate the core specification and implementation. However, employees are complicated. To ensure that they use the new approach, you may need to take into account variations in employment regulation and culture. In effect, you need to balance compliance with some degree of sensitivity to local issues.

Any one of our four types of project could be used for a project of this nature, but the results will probably be very different:

• A Type 1 project, in which the project team was staffed by internal people and consultants from just one country, would result in absolute consistency across all countries but the new processes and systems will be resented by those who have to use them, so implementation is likely to be more expensive and less effective than hoped, but it will at least be completed, and probably on time and within budget.

• A Type 2 project, where the internal people came from one country but the consultants came from different ones, would probably be the worst possible choice. The internal staff would not be aware of the variations in different countries; that means they would not be able to alert the consultants to potential issues or help the consultants deal with them as they arose. Furthermore, because the consultants come from different parts of the world, they are unlikely to find it easy to adopt a single approach. As soon as they encounter resistance from individual countries, they will empathise with the local employees and will champion the changes that the latter would like to include rather than reducing them. In these circumstances, the project would over-run substantially; indeed, there is a danger that it would never be completed as neither the client's people nor the consultants would be able to draw a line at which the level of customisation stops. The most probable scenario is that parts of the new processes and systems would be implemented in some countries, but that the overall project would rumble on for years, with constant adjustments being made.

- A Type 4 project, staffed by clients and consultants from many countries, would be most effective at understanding the nuances in each local operation but would be hopelessly inadequate when it comes to pulling them together into a single process and system. Each country's team would work independently and the level of commonality between their approaches would be minimal. As a result, new processes and systems would be implemented, perhaps even on time and budget, but they would fail to achieve the overall objective: each country would have its own approach.

- In these circumstances, a Type 3 project makes the most sense. By using a team of consultants from one (or similar) countries and/or cultures, you are far more likely to achieve a single, consistent set of processes and systems at the end than if you pulled together a team of consultants who reflected the diversity of your HR operations. However, by using a team of people from your organisation that do understand the differences, you can balance the need for compliance with an acknowledgement that some, probably cosmetic and quite limited aspects of the new processes and systems, can be tailored to the needs of individual countries without compromising its overall integrity.

Every approach has its strengths and weaknesses

Tensions almost inevitably exist in projects such as this. At a fundamental level, they are about power: the ability of local operations to operate and take decisions independently in a world in which the corporate centre is taking an increasingly interventionist role. A Type 3 project has the critical advantage in that it brings that tension inside the project. The consultants, coming from a single culture, are playing the part of the corporation's headquarters, driving through a single standard. The client team, because they come from different countries or cultures, are in effect the representatives of the company's local operations. By bringing them together, you are forcing them to identify the potential problems and resolve them: sometimes the consultants will win, ensuring that the core of the approach remains consistent across all geographies; sometimes the client staff will win, ensuring that important national differences are taken into account where possible. Inevitably, there will be clashes between the two sides: the consultants will become frustrated by the extent of changes and complications introduced by the internal staff; the internal staff, for their part, will resent the consultants' single-minded pursuit of consistency. However, providing that their overall goal is clear and that they are motivated to achieve it, they will resolve such issues between themselves rather than within the wider organisation.

It should go without saying that all four types of project need conventional project management skills: a formal plan; clearly-defined tasks and division of responsibilities; and consistent bottom-up reporting and top-down monitoring. For Type 1 projects, this will be sufficient, but the other types require additional effort.

The problems that arise in a Type 2 project are largely ones of credibility and communication: misunderstandings between the consultants and the client staff; perhaps resentment on the client side that consultants are being flown in from all corners of the world at the client's expense. These relatively minor problems can be dealt with by ensuring that the people from the client side understand why the skills of the consultant are required (a theme we will keep coming back to during the course of this book) and ensuring the consultants concerned demonstrate that specialist knowledge at an early stage, thus earning the respect of those around them. Any other complications that arise from bringing people in from different parts of the world and ensuring that they can work effectively together are for the consulting firm to solve: if problems in the team dynamics do arise, they should not be apparent to the client and it is the responsibility of the consulting firm to solve them.

Types 3 and 4 projects require a different approach, however, one that acknowledges and accommodates local variations where possible. As with the composition of the client-consultant team working on the project, there needs to be a balance between consistency and diversity. The project plan plays just as important a role here, but it may make more sense to break the project up into discrete, relatively autonomous units and to allow each team the freedom to develop their own plans and ways of working, so long as they meet certain unequivocal deadlines and objectives. To this extent, the consulting team should be a microcosm of how the organisation as a whole wants to be managed: the balance of standardisation to customisation desired by the organisation should be mirrored, not only in the type of project structure adopted, but also in the way in which the project is managed, as Figure 6 summarises.

Figure 6: Matching management type of project and project management style to objectives

Type of project	Objectives	Composition of team	Project management style
Type 1	Standardisation and compliance	Homogenous group of client staff and consultants	Conventional top-down management of a single, integrated team
Type 2	Specialist expertise from different countries/cultures	Homogenous group of client staff working with a heterogeneous group of consultants	Conventional top-down management of a single, integrated team
Type 3	Negotiated balance between head-office objectives and the needs of local operations	Homogenous group of consultants working with a heterogeneous group of internal staff	Autonomous teams working closely together and reporting through a single structure
Type 4	Accomodation, even exploitation, of difference	Homogenous group of client staff and consultants	Autonomous teams working independently and coordinated through metrics (eg deadlines and objectives) rather than a single hierarchy

The danger, of course, is that the type of project and style of project management be chosen based on the status quo or on misunderstanding. A homogeneous project team is established to launch a new product in several different markets, or a heterogeneous team is forced to adopt a single, top-heavy governance structure. Even worse, a head-office that has very little central control in practice tries to set up a Type 1 project, a cultural anathema to its local offices around the world. In such circumstances, the consulting project becomes a magnet for wider organisational tensions. The key to managing multinational projects, therefore, lies in not trying to use the project as a means to alter a company's culture or structure, but to see it – and manage it – as a manifestation of that culture.

In summary

International consulting projects fall into four groups, depending on whether the resources supplied by the consulting firm and the client are heterogeneous (bringing different people from different countries and backgrounds) or homogeneous (using people from the same country and similar backgrounds). The most challenging ones to manage are those that contain heterogeneity from one side (the client or the consultant) and homogeneity from the other, as it is almost inevitable that tensions will arise between the two. However, each type of project has its place and the key to success is to choose a structure, team composition and project management style which most closely meets your objectives.

Case study
INBEV – INTERNATIONAL

InBev, the world largest brewer, initiated a large scale project to rationalise their business services in Europe into shared services centres based in Prague and Budapest. This required all enquiries and requests to be managed within a standard set of business processes and one single application.

InBev needed expert help in implementing the solution to several European countries including Germany, Belgium, Luxembourg, United Kingdom, Czech Republic, Hungary and the Netherlands.

Mixed clients and Logica teams managed to:

• Develop the programme management framework and project plans (including risk management)

• Liaise with and manage the vendor development team based in Canada

• Manage the data acquisition, cleansing and preparation processes

• Ensure timely and clear communications to manage stakeholder expectations

• Develop transition plans to bring the main application into Logica support

The programme delivered the required functionality to support the needs for over 500,000 individual accounts across Europe.

InBev is now able to respond to all requests in the native language of the requestor through 150 call centre agents. This has led to a significant reduction in costs and improved customer service levels.

France: maturing relationships

In 2010, the French consulting market is characterised by a belated aware-ness and the will to make up for lost time as regards the management of major transformation programmes linked to the information system.

How has this situation come about? There are two main causes: the first is the dominant position of the Big Four in the 1990s and at the start of the 2000s, which has resulted in almost exclusive importance being given to management consulting; the second is the arrival of the first waves of deregulation in Anglo-Saxon countries, generating these types of project, well before France itself became involved.

Management consulting in the French market is consequently more upstream than elsewhere. Furthermore, in spite of a slightly distant rela-tionship with technology, the search for growth opportunities has led French consulting firms to recognise the importance of information system consulting and to get more involved in assisting businesses in this field.

A client-consultant relationship revitalised by purchasing

In France, consulting had long lived off the historic links which it had with auditing: fees weren't negotiated, competitive bidding was limited and consultants were approached as soon as a study emerged. With globalisation and the hyper-competitiveness which it engenders in times of growth and recession alike, the pressure on costs has become constant; structurally, it is accompanied by the development of the purchasing function, which calls into question the very reasons why businesses turn to consultants. These days, it is necessary to provide evidence of the added value of a study, only approaching an outside consulting firm in the event that the required skills are not available in-house, while at the end of the assignment it is necessary to demonstrate the return on investment and how it will be generated, in addition to committing to the results.

Furthermore, businesses generally tend to maintain control over the projects that they undertake, sometimes confining, intentionally or otherwise, the consultant's role to the contribution of expertise. They try to use a consulting firm to acquire expertise, know-how, a methodological approach and perhaps even to compare it with their own practices. Consequently, the commitment to deliverables is not as important as one might have thought.

The difficulty of consulting practised in this way lies in the fact that the assignments are generally short and involve the image of a client within his own company. The search for effectiveness must be permanent and the support immediately taken away because rectifying a situation will always prove more complex in a consulting assignment than in the framework of a project, where time provides greater room for manoeuvre. In the words of Benoît Leboucher, a member of the Sourcing team at Logica Business Consulting: "Consulting is like rock-climbing. You have to keep raising yourself up, without falling into the abyss and dragging the rest of the roped party down with you."

"Selling consulting is about inspiring trust," he continues. This trust is the basis of a strong bond which forms between businesses and consulting firms, a bond which purchasing departments try to weaken in order to restrict the emotional aspect of the relationship and to mediate using more factual, tangible elements.

An historic link between project ownership and project management

Inspired by the model of Buildings and Public Works, which is also manifested in other contexts, the French consulting market has long observed a fairly monolithic dichotomy between project ownership and project management, essentially for ethical reasons. Due to the absence of a conflict of interest between the two parties the situation remains healthy but reveals a certain rigidity which contrasts with the flexibility required in the economy of the 2010s.

As a result we have observed the introduction of sometimes subtle nuances in this model and the emergence of new practices, such as the emergence of transversal project owners, capable of formulating statements of requirements in emerging domains where technological expertise is indispensable. This is something we have seen several times in different business sectors, in very diverse fields such as data exchange management or real-time business monitoring.

Purchasing strategies which go beyond the mere observance of a strict project ownership/project management dichotomy are progressively being implemented, except at public sector level.

The upstream/downstream approach is being revitalised: businesses will try to have upstream processes performed by smaller consulting firms that have a reputation for expertise and entrust the implementation phase to companies with greater financial muscle, which are capable of carrying out assignments on a fixed rate basis. However, the large consulting firms need to give credibility to their expertise, which means that they also position themselves upstream. They will then bring content to their clients, by adapting certain media to the business world which are usually reserved for other uses, e.g. Web TV, social networks......

A more mature relationship

Over time, French businesses have entered into a more mature relationship with the consulting world. They have come to appreciate the contribution that a consultant makes and understand the role that they must themselves play with regard to consultants. As a result, consultants are less exposed than in the past, while also being more empowered with responsibility in their specialist fields. On the other hand, the sponsorship of consulting firms has weakened and the client often retains operational control over projects.

Clients are slightly less inclined to hire "big names", although they still make a personal commitment to the selections that they make. Even if a company is small in size, it can be hired purely on the basis of its image and expertise, which reinforces the fact that, ultimately, little control is entrusted to the external consultancies. The upstream positioning reinforces its credibility and expertise. The quality of the engagement remains decisive.

The decision to launch a consulting project has become more democratic. It is no longer the exclusive responsibility of top management but is directed at middle management. As a result, for a consulting firm, the management of contacts in the business must become diversified. It has become essential to make oneself known and to stay close to all levels of the client's business. In this sense, it is easy to understand the emerging importance of Internet media in the relationship between consultancies and businesses.

The use of external services generates flexibility in a market where hiring and firing remains problematic. This explains the success of the major French service providers. Consulting firms regulate the job market. Almost paradoxically, we see interim management offerings emerging in certain consulting firms, both in France and abroad. In fact, during times of economic crisis, voluntary redundancy plans result in a loss of expertise in certain companies. At the earliest signs of recovery, it is necessary to make up for this loss, leading inevitably to the use of consultancy firms.

The transfer of expertise benefits from the concept of immersion and the proliferation of joint teams. In return, business and consulting firms must make an extra effort in preparing project plans and in acquiring the necessary in-house experience.

The UK: the mid-Atlantic approach

The distinctive characteristics of the UK consulting industry

In terms of the client-consultant relationship, the United Kingdom (like the country itself) lies somewhere between the United States and Europe. Historic trading patterns, inward investment and the presence of many US-owned and multinational firms, has brought the influence of American-style management. Indeed, the arrival of so many US businesses after the Second World War meant that the UK also became the launch-pad for the US consultancies which, by the 1950s, were looking to establish bases in Europe. This early boost to the UK consulting industry, combined with an Anglo-Saxon predisposition to see business as a set of scientific principles and tools that could be taken from one organisation to another, means that the country is still the second biggest market for consulting after Germany. In common with US companies, those in the UK simply make greater and more regular use of consultants than those of almost any other nationality.

Moreover, it is not just that UK companies use more consultants more often, but that they are willing to use them in a wide range of different activities. Unlike in France, where there is a clear distinction between the strategy and/or design elements of a consulting assignment and the actual implementation, the border between these services in the UK is much more permeable. This has resulted in a greater number of firms which are able to straddle the two types of work and means that "operational" consulting, focused on improving the performance of an organisation, IT consulting and large-scale programme management, are all particularly strong and growing markets (Figure 7).

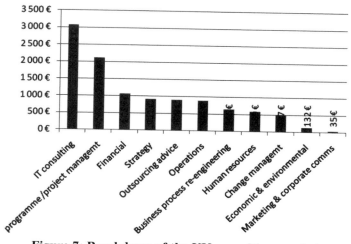

**Figure 7: Breakdown of the UK consulting market
by service in 2008 (€ms)**

The blurred distinction between strategy and execution has had two other, important implications. First, it has increased the average size of projects in the UK, as firms have been able – often encouraged, in fact – to implement their recommendations. Consulting firms in the UK, or the UK divisions of international firms, tend to be bigger than in most other countries as a result, and the distance between these very large firms and the next tier of firms is particularly wide. Second, it has meant that a wide range of companies offer consulting services, not just consulting firms. As Figure 8 indicates, there are some firms that only offer traditional ("pure") management consulting, ranging from the very large to small boutiques. As in other countries, the audit and accounting firms offer consultancy: typically, their consulting practices in the UK are larger, relative to their other business lines, than in continental Europe. There is also a group of very large firms offering consulting alongside outsourcing and IT work, as there is elsewhere in Europe. However, the UK consulting industry has other significant segments: IT, outsourcing and engineering firms, all of which have a distinctive presence in the industry and all of which bridge the gap between strategy and implementation.

Be advised

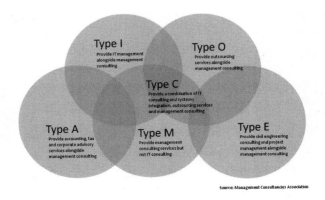

Figure 8: Segmenting the management and IT consulting industry

The other distinctive thing about the UK consulting market is the relative importance of two sectors: financial services and the public sector, each of which respectively account for around a quarter and a third of all money spent on consulting in the UK.

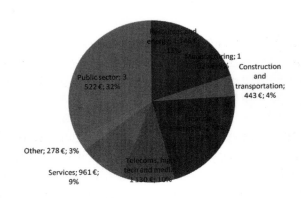

**Figure 9: Breakdown of the UK consulting market
by sector in 2008 (€ms)**

The financial services sector has been a crucible of innovation for both itself and its suppliers. It has been at the forefront of many of the trends discussed below and the way in which it plans to change the way it uses consultants in the future may tell us a great deal about long-term trends in the consulting industry as a whole. The public sector, too, has been a source of innovation, although this is a much more recent phenomenon. Under pressure from politicians since the mid-1990s, government departments have been restructuring and modernising the services they provide. This process has required new technology and specialist skills, much of which has been provided by consulting firms. As a result, the early years of the millennium saw public sector expenditure on consultants more than double.

These three structural and cultural differences – the blurred boundary between strategy and execution, the range of different firms offering consulting services and the importance of the financial and public sectors – go some way towards accounting for the distinctive characteristics of the way UK clients buy and use consultants.

Using consultants in the UK

The presence of multinational corporations, innovation from financial institutions and the important role the public sector plays all mean that the buying of consulting services has changed dramatically in the UK over the last ten years.

The rise of the procurement manager, whose remit is to step in between consulting firm and their client, has threatened the two thirds of revenue UK consulting firms typically win from existing clients. Better information about market conditions and more aggressive negotiating tactics have also kept prices depressed, even, as during 2004-08, when levels of demand had reached record highs. However, perhaps the most significant impact of more formal procurement processes has been to limit the number of options that can be explored between clients and consultants both prior to and during the sales cycle. Winning work is now often a laborious and expensive process for UK consulting firms, expenditure that has to be recouped by keeping prices high where possible. Luckily, prices in the UK consulting industry are among the highest in the world, if not the highest. This means that, while the margins of consulting firms in the country have deteriorated since the Millennium, they still tend to be higher than elsewhere in Europe.

Large multinational corporations have been at the forefront of setting up preferred supplier lists and, because many of them have regional headquarters in the UK, this practice is now spreading rapidly throughout domestic firms as well. Not surprisingly, consulting firms that have been successful in winning places on such lists view the trend comparatively positively; those that have not been successful are entirely negative. Whatever the subjective view, preferred supplier lists pose a huge challenge for UK-based firms, potentially polarising the industry further into the haves and the have-nots.

Furthermore, the apparently inexorable rise of professionalised procurement and preferred supplier lists has some unintended consequences. Despite the comparatively high prices associated with consulting services in the UK, there is evidence that some consulting services are becoming commoditised. As the opportunity for consultants to talk to clients about their brief and to understand where they can add most value is squeezed by the procurement rules, the chances of being able to add value thus diminish in practice. Moreover, the focus on cost deflects the debate away from the value they can genuinely add. As a result, fee rates have barely recovered since they plunged at the end of the dotcom boom and margins are falling. Furthermore, while demand for consulting has increased, there has been no concurrent improvement in the reputation of consultants. Despite research by the industry, the reputation of the consulting industry, certainly as portrayed in the media, is largely negative.

All of this, combined with the economic downturn, means that expenditure on consultants in the UK is being scrutinised as never before. So what are clients looking for? Like clients everywhere, the top of their agenda is to get the work they have commissioned completed to their satisfaction, on time and within the agreed budget. Perhaps because of the influence of US-inspired management techniques and business schools and because of this blurred boundary between strategy and execution, UK clients also think it is important for a consulting firm to have a methodology. Knowing that a firm has completed a similar assignment, ideally in the same sector, gives them confidence. One of the implications of this is that a firm's brand and reputation is crucial in its ability be on the long list for a piece of work. Relationships do matter, especially in the closing stages of the sales cycle, but are usually not sufficient to get a firm automatic access to work, especially in areas where the client has not used them before. Innovation and creativity are usually high on UK clients' official agenda, but they it is questionable how important these facets are to them in practice. Matched against their desire for tried-and-tested methodologies, it is hard to believe that they truly want to be leading-edge. Instead, one suspects, they are looking for assurance that the consultants' methodology, while critical to the latter's ability to win work, will not be applied too rigidly in practice.

The emphasis on methodologies has another impact. If an individual is trained in a specific firm's approach (or, in the case of the public sector, a specific client's approach), then they can take that know-how else-where, treating it as quasi qualification. This means that an individual consultant is less tied to their firm than they might be elsewhere: during the previous major downturn in the consulting industry before the current one, in 2002-03, large-scale consulting firms reacted to falling demand and excess capacity by making sizeable groups of people redundant, inadvertently populating the market with people who had all the training of a consultant in a bigger firm but charge out their time at a fraction of the rate. Clients, especially centralised procurement departments look-ing to cut costs, seized this opportunity, creating a significant market for independent and freelance consultants. Although the current downturn may be changing this slightly – freelancers are now a key target for cutbacks – the UK continues to have a large number of independent consultants. Because of this, it also has a wide variety of consulting firm structures: competing with the traditional "pyramid-shaped" firms, are virtual firms employing only a handful of people while the consultants are employed on a loose, "associate" basis. Co-operation and collaboration between consulting firms, especially the small and mid-sized players, are strong as well.

Such a structure creates opportunities for clients, the more sophisticated among whom are now looking to see what the next evolutionary step in buying consulting will be. Rather than expecting a single big firm on their preferred supplier list to provide all the resources a given project requires by itself, these clients will either bring in smaller, specialist firms to work alongside them, or – perhaps more probably – put the firms under pressure to use a variety of different sources, not just their own people. Like clients across the globe, UK clients are intensely interested in specialist skills – the UK Management Consultancies Association estimates that around half of all projects are triggered by this need – and they want to be able to access world-class expertise wherever they see it. For the consulting firms, this creates both a challenge and an opportunity: although they may need to experiment with different and more innovative organisational models, they may find themselves orchestrating the resources of their rivals.

However, the importance of structured methodologies in the UK consulting market does not mean that relationships are not important. If anything, the recent recession has strengthened managers' preference for working with people they know they can trust, so relationships have enjoyed a renaissance. This is not confined to the sales process: if you ask a UK client what characterises the best consulting projects in their experience, they will almost always refer to the sense of partnership they had, in which the consultants and clients worked seamlessly together as an integrated team. It is therefore the norm in the UK for consultants to work on their clients' sites, not in their own offices, and for clients to provide some of their own staff to work alongside the consultants. Governance and reporting structures can be onerous, especially in the public sector, although most of those involved would acknowledge that it is still their ability to work together effectively that sees them through the problems that arise.

But perhaps the biggest challenge facing both clients and consultants in the UK is how to reconcile these two ways of thinking: the methodology-led approach with the acknowledgement that strong working relationships remain fundamental to success in consulting. Procurement rules may be pushing the consulting industry towards ever more commoditisation, but personal chemistry continues to add value. These dilemmas are coalescing around one issue: how to measure the value consultants add. Despite their structured, sometimes regimented approach to buying consulting, few UK clients have historically put much effort into measuring consultants' contribution, especially once the latter have left. Increasing scrutiny of decisions to bring consultants in is changing that, with organisations asking consultants to estimate the return on investment for their work. Consulting firms are responding by stressing their willingness to be paid on a risk-reward basis and by becoming more systematic when it comes to evaluating their work once it is finished by surveying their clients' satisfaction. This process is in its infancy, and both sides have much to consider and learn before a meaningful solution can be found. However, it promises to be the dominant issue in the UK consulting industry for the foreseeable future.

Wiltshire Council case study

The last decade has seen significant change in local government in the UK, including, in some areas, bringing together the services delivered separately by county and district councils under a new, single, unitary council. In 2007, Wiltshire County Council, succeeded in its bid to establish a new unitary "Wiltshire Council" to deliver the full range of services provided by the County Council and four district councils.

In addition to improving service delivery and democratic engagement for communities across Wiltshire, one of the objectives in doing this has been to save money: the new, Wiltshire Council is able to combine the five previously separate back-office and support functions, enabling it to deliver better services to communities whilst keeping council tax levels under control. However, like all restructuring, change brought an opportunity to do things differently.

Wiltshire Council estimated that it could save around £9 million a year from a mix of greater efficiency and better procurement. It therefore embarked on an ambitious 13-month programme to implement an entire suite of integrated back-office systems, covering human resources, payroll, finance and procurement – called the Business Management Programme - as part of the One Council for Wiltshire work.

Logica took on the overall management of the BMP, including the transition and change management needed to move to a shared services arrangement in which all parts of the new council would access one central point for internal support. This was by no means "just" a large-scale IT enabled change programme – although even that by itself was complicated enough – but would require new ways of working and new behaviours across the whole of the new organisation – but especially for the 350 people in the new shared services team. Rather than seeing these people as simple support staff, Wiltshire wanted to nurture professionalism and make its corporate services a centre of excellence.

"That's what we're working on now," says Phil Barnett, Head of Local Government for Logica in the UK. "Our role is to deliver, not just the transformation Wiltshire Council is looking for, but an SAP template for local government as a whole. The challenges Wiltshire is responding too are by no means unique: every council is under massive pressure to do more with less and shared services and new back-office systems are fundamental to being able to achieve this. But our work is not just about the technology: we have to help the Council create a single team that will drive change forward internally. "

The project began in March 2008 and went live on the 1st April 2009. "We've had five months of safe running since then," comments Barnett, "and we're well on track to delivering the anticipated benefits." Indeed, benefits "realisation" – ensuring that the savings identified in Wiltshire's original business case do come through in practice – has been an important aspect of Logica's role. "Lot of organisations invest considerable time and effort in putting together business cases, only to take their eye off the ball when it comes to delivering the expected savings," says Barnett. A key obstacle is that organisations do not always know what their starting point is, so measuring improvement is difficult. "Our first step in situation such as this is to identify the baseline of current costs. This allows us to measure not only the impact the changes will have but also the relative importance of each element of the change. What costs are associated with what processes? How much of the anticipate savings can be attributed to the implementation of a new system, and how much to changing the way people work? Which people should be redeployed? Analysis such as this puts the project sponsor in the driving seat. It gives them the information they need to work with their peers and confirm where savings will be made, that, if such and such a system is changed, that so many people will be released, and so on."

Ensuring that that the whole business bought into the programme as another key aspect of Logica's work, so the firm created a "business change network", a group of people – change champions and agents – who between them represented the sub-groups in each line of business and who could be used as conduits of information to the business as a whole. "When you go live on the first day of a programme as complex as this, you can have people turning round and saying they don't know what's happening and they can't do their jobs," says Barnett. "You have to ensure that every avenue of communication has been used but, even more importantly, that people within the business are accountable for ensuring the messages have got across."

Looking back on the programme, Barnett believes there have been two critical factors in making it a success. The first was genuine engagement among the senior people in Wiltshire Council: "The programme sponsor recognised from the outset that this would be half his job going forward and that he had to take an active role in almost every aspect. He also worked hard to ensure that all the other executive directors understood what was going on and were in a position to take informed decisions about the project. He lived and breathed the programme."

The second success factor was the client-consultant relationship. Rather than being treated as a mere contractor, Logica was seen as the leader of the programme, given equal access to important discussions and decisions. "I went to every programme board," recalls Barnett, "but also had direct access to the programme's sponsor, so issues could be dealt instantly. Of the 200 people involved in the project, around 80 of them came from Logica, but we had a say in how all these resources were used. We also learnt quickly not to be high-handed about this: we wanted to keep the momentum going, but we also wanted to ensure that everyone came with us. The people we worked with there were very competent, but they needed our experience from other, similar projects, so the relationship was very much one of partnership. We each brought different qualities and knowledge to make it a success."

Germany: experience balanced with innovation

Selection of consultants and purchasing processes

The German consulting market reflects the distribution of the main economic sites in the country. Unlike other countries, such as France, Portugal or The Netherlands, for which their capital area provides the geographical focal point for economy, in Germany, projects take place around several economic centres, such as Hamburg, Frankfurt, Ludwigshafen or Munich. Thus a consulting company should be situated in several locations all over Germany, if they aim to decrease travel expenses.

By way of introduction, it appears that the use of consulting services differs markedly according to the size of the business. Small and medium-sized businesses often try to staff projects with their own resources, whereas large businesses tend to view consulting as a contribution of expertise, as well as one of flexibility. In this respect, the client businesses keeps strategic analysis in-house, then outsources the implementation to consulting firms, hoping to benefit from state-of-the-art, specialist and innovative procedures: it is easier to understand in this context why IT consulting and technological innovation have come to occupy a prominent position in consulting professions.

Nevertheless, and although it might seem paradoxical within an innovative framework, the selection process remains dependent on expertise acquired in other similar contexts, and references are essential in this regard. It is important that the consulting firm is able to continually update and improve its know-how and practices.

The level of decision-making remains linked to the responsibilities of the programme under consideration: the more strategic the project, the higher up the decision of whether and how to use consulting services is made. This is especially true in the case of business or management consulting, since IT consulting is directed more at middle management, in connection with the finance department.

Just as in other European countries, purchasing processes have become more professionalised, progressively moving away from the realm of negotiated contracts towards centralised procurement policies, with an increased demand for fixed-price services in order to keep a tighter control over commitments (costs, timescales and quality). However, there still remains a certain lack of maturity as regards the initial statement of requirements, which is a guarantee of the levels of conformity and quality obtained.

Expectations

When the choice is open, two major criteria influence the decision:

• The application of innovation

• The consultants' experience in an equivalent or closely related field explains why clients turn to professionals with several years' experience in the profession

The combination of these two factors determines the model consultant in the eyes of the business. Someone whose expertise is based on past experience, who is always ready to think out of the box, who is always on the move and never standing still. It is interesting to note that, in Germany, experience means being flexible.

Innovation and flexibility clearly distinguish consulting practices in Germany and explain why overly rigid methodologies only rarely apply to this type of assignment, which is offset by rigorous project management and the use of precise metrics for measuring the success of the operation.

Pricing remains an important factor, especially during times of economic crisis, but is perhaps less decisive than the previous two criteria: this is explained by the importance of proximity in the client-consultant relationship (see below). It demonstrates that loyalty is likely to increase if the relationship is one of trust, since it can rise above purely client/supplier considerations to forge another, more durable type of relationship.

Due to the great diversity of tasks entrusted to a consulting firm, adaptation of the consultant's know-how to the context and the assignment takes precedence and can only be observed in the field.

The client-consultant relationship

During consulting assignments, an individual relationship is formed between a consultant and his client, which ultimately goes beyond the framework that the purchasing department tries to limit. As we have been able to observe, especially in Germany, the success of the consulting assignment depends on the establishment of a relationship of trust. In this context, the relationship takes on multiple dimensions and, regardless of the role played by the consultant, the degree of proximity is what counts.

Consultants join the client's teams in accordance with the principle of immersion, which is widely applied nowadays, including across the Atlantic.

As regards the implementation of complex, innovative projects, it is noticeable that clients appreciate the ability to organise mixed teams, equipped with a business component and an IT component. This is in order to ensure fluency in the diversification of issues, to improve the quality of the service, and to prevent the client's teams from being overloaded by the consulting teams, generally to communicate knowledge already formalised elsewhere. Having embarked on such a project, the business consultants will ultimately have the task of ensuring the functional transfer of expertise by the IT consultants.

Getting value

A successful service must include several aspects. Firstly, it must not be "autocentric". Beyond the job itself, being carried out to a high standard, the client expects a wider, more open analysis which potentially opens up new perspectives. He is also hoping to be told the truth, even if it isn't always pleasant to hear. Because these points are not subject to any measurement, the payment of a consulting service is not really dependent on performance indicators.

Case study

DAIMLER - GREEN IT

The Green IT project at Daimler was an ambitious, groundbreaking project of major proportions. It also presented numerous challenges, the first of which was to build the company's IT infrastructure so as to preserve the environment and use resources sparingly throughout the entire lifecycle of the hardware, while also supporting the creation of IT solutions so that they themselves contribute to this strategy of sustainability.

All aspects of the information system were involved in this operation: consequent usage and spread of virtualisation technologies to optimise the use of machines, the rolling out of communication technologies to facilitate teamwork and reduce legwork. Continuous monitoring of power consumption by printers, desktop and laptop computers and finally an extensive in-house communication programme to raise awareness about the issues behind the project.

The Logica Business Consulting team played a particularly active role as part of the Daimler Project Management Office (PMO) it devised the solutions, it fine-tuned them by comparing them with the client's economic and technological environment, before submitting them to the client, up to the point where, once the solutions had been validated by both parties, an outreach programme could be implemented a true incubator approach.

Daimler distributed information via multiple channels, thereby assuring more expansive and consistent change management. The importance of this communication called for a constant onsite presence.

Innovation, project management and change management: as part of Daimler PMO, Logica Business Consulting defined many aspects of this programme and tackled them head on for the benefit of Daimler, which estimates to have saved 4 million euros, 40 million kWh of power and cut its CO_2 emissions by 25,000 tonnes, with specific reference to the balanced scorecard indicators monitoring the success of the program in the future. The assignment was a resounding success, which explains the subsequent proliferation of communication operations, this time external, between Logica Business Consulting and its client.

The Nordics:
relationships remain important

Sweden

Due to the increasing maturity shown by clients in recent years, the Swedish consulting market appears to have become very competitive. All large Swedish businesses make extensive use of consulting services and are used to having consultants integrated into their teams.

As a result, all of the market's major consulting players have also set up local offices. Considering the consumer behaviour of clients and the wide choice available to them, it is difficult to differentiate oneself and carve out an original niche in the market. The decision to hire a consulting firm has little to do with the firm and its offering. Rather, the references and background of the consultants are what make the difference during the purchasing process, as well as the ability to demonstrate a return on investment from a business point of view.

Consulting in Sweden is focused as much on business as it is on technology and, just as in other countries, consultancies try to find the best way to bridge the gap between the former and the latter, which in reality becomes one of the best ways of differentiating themselves. Consulting firms are looking for the best ways to offer their clients a one-stop shop. A position as trusted advisor will probably be more difficult to achieve, given that consultants are valued for their interchangeability.

As in all other countries, purchasing departments are increasingly involved and master agreements have become decisive as a means of staying close to the end client, which is just as important as anywhere else. Reversed auctions have in the past caused more damage than progress, to the extent that numerous clients have turned away from this type of practice and now recognise that a minimum price must be set. Among the numerous levels of decision-making, the Swedish market is distinguished by a small peculiarity: trade unions are entitled to their say in the process. Similarly, they generally also play a part in project steering committees.

There is an equal preference for results-based contracts on the one hand and time-and-materials contracts on the other. Thus it is not uncommon to find all-in assignments in which the consulting firm is given a high level of responsibility and overall control of autonomous teams, just as it is common to find client/consultant teams controlled by the client. Taking into account the size of the market, a failing assignment or project will have less overall impact for the players involved than would be the case in smaller markets. Nevertheless, just as everywhere else, the relationship between client and consulting firm will be considerably damaged and will have to be rebuilt.

The bulk of the consulting market is based around Stockholm, although certain large offshore clients ask for a local presence.

In order to limit the risk, certain large projects are split so that a relationship can be maintained.

In terms of methodology, clients don't necessarily ask for dedicated frameworks. This must be related to the assumed interchangeability of consultants, who are seen more as expertise providers in a given field. It is therefore up to the consultant to demonstrate his/her ability to adapt to the methodology used by a given business (except perhaps as regards medium-sized businesses, which will expect the consulting firm to take more initiative in their field of expertise). On this basis, communication remains the key to a successful consulting assignment.

Sweden has always maintained a very strong relationship with technology and clients willingly put themselves forward as early adopters who are difficult to deter. As a result, the sole difficulty lies in the commitment that a consulting firm can make with a client, with regards to an emerging technology, as they are not always well-established and therefore lacking experts and even a critical mass of expertise. There again, communication inevitably plays a key role.

The transfer of expertise is a key criterion in selecting a consulting firm for results-based projects. The ability to assemble joint teams right from day one, including on predominantly results-based projects, is highly sought after.

In view of all these aspects, consulting firms are required to offer very specific, standardised expertise which takes into account all of the afore-mentioned criteria: appetite for technology, ability to adapt to an existing methodology, continuous transfer of expertise. In itself, this expertise already resembles a genuine methodology.

Finally it must be noted that the distribution of expertise within a consulting firm in Sweden does not resemble a pyramid but rather a diamond. Young people entering the job market don't spontaneously embark on a consulting career, instead choosing to do so after having accumulated several years of professional experience.

Finland

The Finnish market contrasts strongly with that of its larger neighbour. There are fewer international businesses, while small and medium-sized businesses are considerably more numerous, with a strong culture of in-house implementation. The latter are naturally less inclined to use consulting services outside of clearly identified contexts, such as the occasional need for specialist expertise.

Besides large corporations, the public sector has also made frequent use of consulting firms. This means that the consulting market is more structured around small and highly specialist studios, rather than large consulting firms. However, the market is growing and developing and the arrival of more established players cannot be ruled out in the relatively short term.

This trend seems to be accompanied by a maturing market in which the role of consultants is becoming diversified and the average duration of assignments is increasing. The purchasing process is also becoming better organised and more specific.

In any case, consulting is still a business in which maintaining a close relationship with clients is vital to growth. Without this proximity, it is almost impossible to carve out a niche in the market. Client relationship management and, to a lesser extent, one's past client portfolio, are primary considerations. This is offset by the fact that a consultant can work long term for a client if his services are considered essential, which contrasts markedly with the situation in Sweden. It is possible to earn the role of trusted advisor, although a consultant must listen closely to his client and continually exceed expectations before being entrusted with this responsibility.

Contracts are mainly on a time-and-materials basis. In the systems, issues such as the transfer of expertise or communication plan management are not really on the agenda. The emphasis is placed more on clarity in the presentation of an analysis, on the pragmatism of conclusions and the understanding of the resulting business benefits. Clients like to associate consulting firms with the achievement of benefits identified by assignments, although they don't yet seem mature enough to really observe this type of performance in the field.

Case study

FINNISH MINISTRY OF FINANCE

The Ministry of Finance had conducted a pre-study on how to further develop available electronic services related to citizens and corporations. The objectives of the project were to capture the business requirements for these services and conceptualise them into a business solution that could be then sourced to potential IT vendors.

Consultants were hired to capture the business needs from different governmental actors and formulate a business vision accordingly. To capture end-user viewpoints and align those with business requirements and review high-level technical architecture opportunities and limitations, as well as to define a preliminary concept for "my e-government e-services" and validate this concept with different stakeholders and selected end-user groups.

Project objectives and consultant involvement was communicated in at least three different ways

1. A main kick-off including all involved stakeholders

2. An early communication plan involving several activities including monthly letters, specific intra pages and other communications

3. Specific workshops held with main parts of the organisation and their stakeholders, to build a vision and a common ground of the programme

Consultants had a very central role together with the client programme management team in all of the above-mentioned three areas. The kick-off was prepared by both teams. A communication plan was built and key messages defined. These messages structured the whole communication at the programme level. Specific workshops were planned and facilitated by key consultants.

Several internal stakeholders were involved in the project, in order to make a comprehensive capture of the requirements and build an accurate business solution concept. The client–consultant relationship was open, and, thanks to this multi-level communication, consultants could operate in trust and autonomy: two key factors for success in the consulting field.

Portugal:
risk and innovation

"The Portuguese consulting market is characterised by its size. Everyone knows each other," explains Paulo Luz, consulting manager at Logica Business Consulting Portugal. "Furthermore, we are a country rooted in Latin culture where proximity, language and informality play a major role." As a result, the dynamic Portuguese market shows some interesting peculiarities, which other nations could draw inspiration from to enrich and diversify their client/consultant relationship.

As has been noted in other countries, the closeness of the client-consultant relationship has taken a new turn as the power of central purchasing departments has increased, to the point where the latter now plays a paramount role in the relationship between consulting firms and their ultimate clients. The exception here is the public sector, where the terms of requests for tenders have long been very structured. Nevertheless, procurement departments cannot supersede the importance of networks of relationships at multiple levels because mutual trust remains the cornerstone of the relationship. Consulting firms must pay attention to nurturing their direct relationship with the client, just as they are obliged to respect and adhere closely to the demands of the purchasing department. Regular and effective account management by dedicated personnel is imperative.

The country's dense economic fabric also explains another phenomenon: the obligation of result which is imposed on consulting firms. When an assignment doesn't achieve results and the client's expectations are not met, word gets around very quickly with potentially damaging consequences for the image of the contracted firm. Therefore to counteract this danger, consultancies very often undertake assignments on a flat-rate fee rather than a time-and-materials basis, demanding to be put in charge of managing their assignments and the related risks.

In this context, the notion of joint client/consultant teams remains pertinent, for reasons other than those observed in France or Germany. In contrast to those markets, flexibility is not emphasised. On the other hand, frequent validation of the intermediate key points with clients avoids the tunnel effect and ensures a steady ship, even when the going gets tough.

The nature of consulting in Portugal

The size of assignments varies and rarely exceeds 200,000 euros. Due to the predominance of flat-rate agreements, it is not uncommon for firms to carry out a succession of small assignments, enabling them to maintain a dynamic model where the contribution of value is constantly reassessed.

Upstream presence does not guarantee downstream presence. In fact, there is a certain amount of pressure on prices. The going rate for operational (non-strategic) consulting, for instance process re-engineering assignments, is not vastly different from that for traditional computer engineering, for example. On average, the difference in fees is in the region of 20% to 25%, although current downward pressure on engineering is bridging this gap.

The contribution of value, mainly via innovation, plays a decisive role in justifying higher-priced services. Consulting firms tend to do this in two ways. They identify emerging ideas which have struck a particular chord with their clients, and as a result, some very "fashionable" fields such as information system modernisation are booming. However, they also build on these initial ideas in the course of assignments, looking at how, for example, new technology such as Web 2.0 and video technologies can be used in practice. Generally speaking, the Portuguese market demonstrates a voracious appetite for innovation and technology, which players in the consulting market must exploit in their proposals in order to convince clients of the relevance of their approach.

Case study

LAND USE PLANNING

The Portuguese ministry responsible for land use planning has its own information system, the quality of which determined how it could be upgraded. Prior to drawing up a strategic IT upgrade plan, the ministry is hoping to carry out a thorough assessment of the system.

The ministry's departments hired Logica Business Consulting for several consulting assignments on a reduced flat-fee basis which were carried out in succession to comprise a complete programme: assessment of data quality, data management methodology, process re-engineering following changes in legislation.

At the same time, Logica deployed its team specialising in geographical information systems to ascertain the viability of integrating these technologies in the client's system and to formulate an integration plan.

The Logica consultants took on the role of trusted adviser to the client's main decision makers. The results of the project were set out in a position paper submitted to senior executives.

The Netherlands: shifting towards technology

The Dutch consulting market is firmly shifting towards IT consulting: "After a first generation of consulting aimed at chief executives and a second, based on Excel spreadsheets, targeting chief finance officers, we are now in the middle of a third wave, which takes into account the growing importance of chief information officers and chief technology officers in the company organisation chart," affirms Geleyn Meijer of Logica's Amsterdam office. For evidence of this, you only need to look at the community web platforms which have emerged enabling CIOs to organise themselves into lobbies. But what does this mean for consulting?

Value proposition and innovation

According to Geleyn Meijer, the key weapon in the consultant's armoury is their value proposition based on models and prototypes. The aim is to convince business departments that they need to address a particular emerging domain and may need to revise their positioning or strategy in relation to this new domain. "Technology merely expedites this value proposition: it is used to support strategy, but it can also lead to the realignment of strategy. Organisations want to reinvent themselves thanks to the information system," says Meijer.

As Frans Dagelet informs us, this shows that the consulting market is conducive to transformation and change, taking it from a "red ocean" approach, in which competition is based on eliminating rivals on a given business terrain, towards a "blue ocean" approach where the key to success is the exploitation of new market spaces large enough to accommodate different competitors, without them necessarily trying to exterminate each other – both concepts are used in marketing theory.

In the context of the Dutch economy, this value proposition consists of determining how to guide a given business toward a service-oriented model. Logica has been able to work in partnership with Rabobank, for example, to construct the prototype of the Service Corner ATM, which provides a central point of access to banking and non-banking services. This upstream positioning enables the consultancy to maintain a position as partner and trusted advisor to its corporate clients.

This is just one example, but the Dutch market has always embraced consultants and made extensive use of them. Vertically, the public sector is particularly buoyant in this respect. Just like a number of industrialised European countries, the health sector must face up to important issues such as the effective management of an ageing population. But Dutch organisations in general have shown themselves to be very receptive to technology and don't hesitate to put new tools to the test. However, they are also not slow to back-pedal if the technology proves to be too immature. Thus, in this respect, there has to be a balance between innovation and established practices.

Engagement and partnership

Due to the long-term partnerships between businesses and consulting firms, more than two-thirds of consulting projects are performed on a time-and-materials basis, with hourly billing. This is different to France, for example, where half-day billing is generally the norm. Few engagements are carried out according to a fixed fee basis, although this billing method is slowly on the increase. It should be noted however that time-and-materials contracting does not exclude the obligation of results.

In fact, Dutch enterprises don't use consultants to make up for the inflexibility of the job market by allocating resources according to need. On the contrary, they tend to engage entire "apparatuses", including management teams, and to empower their partner with responsibility even though the type of contract they adopt does not seem to lend itself to this approach. Any failure is severely punished by the clients, who then don't hesitate to call into question partnerships which have been patiently built up year after year. This is without considering the potential negative effects on the image and reputation of the consulting firm if the failure is made known beyond the confines of the business.

Logica estimates that strategic innovation consulting will continue to operate in a slightly different, supporting role, with clients requesting information without necessarily having a precise target, which would otherwise result in concrete deliverables and a fixed timescale. This way of doing things contrasts sharply with methods observed elsewhere, such as in the French market, where in this type of project, clients are more likely to impose budgetary constraints at the very least, so as to fix a horizon in the absence of a target.

The Dutch approach also displays the principles of partnership, trust and, consequently, limited risk. Clients work with a consulting firm not on the strength of its name or reputation but because it offers the required expertise and because a business manager or associate maintains a relationship of trust with his client.

The consequences for operating procedures

Their mode of engagement can also explain the limited role assigned to skills transfer, which seems to be the weak link for consulting in the Netherlands. There are certainly comprehensive offerings in terms of change management but the integration of this know-how in the aforementioned consulting apparatuses, on innovation projects for example, is not particularly apparent.

In large-scale innovation programmes, the empowered consulting teams are in full partnership with all of the client's teams. In the case of Logica, this has resulted in joint teams on programmes such as those linked to the Rabobank ATM system and the design of services for Vodafone or health services for Philips. In the same way, the client's teams traditionally bring to the table a contextual knowledge of their profession and of how best to approach it.

Generally speaking, the relationship with the purchasing department is growing just as it is in other countries. The early drafting of a master agreement makes it possible to maintain a significant relationship with the end customer, who remains the preferred contact.

The success fee approach is still underdeveloped and consulting firms are rarely interested in performance benefits which may be generated by the effective application of their vision.

Case study
A DUTCH WATER CONSORTIUM

In the Netherlands, a group of companies linked to the water sector formed a consortium, with the aim of establishing services which would be used and shared by these companies and which would enable them to reduce their operating costs. Logica's teams in the Netherlands and Portugal pooled their activities to organise and implement this innovative project, based on Oracle technologies.

In this type of project it is important for the assignment, team motivation and trust, that each consultant remains visible and is placed in close contact with the client, so that the contribution value of the various players is clearly established and recognised. In our case, Logica's Portuguese team had significant business knowledge about the subject, which resulted in the Dutch team drawing on its expertise. As such, it would be difficult to imagine the Portuguese team not being put into direct contact with the client.

Conclusion

A checklist for clients

The purpose of this final chapter is to bring together all the thinking from this book and convert it into a relatively straight-forward and, we hope, very practical list of actions for clients. Some of them are things you might ask the consulting firms you work with to do differently, but most are things your organisation needs to do itself. If we recall the advice of Machiavelli, quoted at the outset of this book, the clever prince can make intelligent use of his advisers, but clever advisers will never make a clever prince.

Before the contract is signed or the project starts:

Objective: To have a clear and fundamental understanding of why you need to bring consultants in and what they can do (the value they can add) which you cannot do with your existing internal resources		
Main barriers to achieving it	**Actions the client can take**	**Actions the consultants can take**
• People leap to the assumption that consultants are required, without looking to see whether the resources required are available within their own organisations • Discussions about why the consultants are necessary happen at too high a level and focus on the immediate issue, rather than on the underlying requirement. Often, insufficient time is dedicated to these discussions	• Start from the assumption that you can do it yourselves, then move on to analysing the benefits consultants would bring (specialist knowledge, process and project management and/or people who can challenge assumptions, manage stakeholders and look from the outside in) • Involve people at all levels in this discussion • Be completely clear why the consultants are necessary and communicate this rationale as widely as possible	• Challenge clients when the latter are not clear about why they cannot do a given piece of work themselves – this is in your own interests as well as your client's: without this understanding, it will be much harder for you to add value

Objective: To draw up a clear, realistic set of requirements that address the end you are trying to get to, rather than the process that may take you there		
Main barriers to achieving it	**Actions the client can take**	**Actions the consultants can take**
• Professional procurement and sales people pulling together request for proposals and the responses to them without an adequate or intimate knowledge of the requirements • Too little involvement from the people who will actually be working on the project, from both the client and consulting side • Clients who draw up their requirements in isolation without getting the input of consulting firms who may have encountered a given issue before	• Ensure there is a dialogue between your end-users and two or three consulting firms that have a track record in the field so that the requirements are developed jointly, taking into account past lessons learned by the consulting firms and constraints you face • Organise workshops and other parts to the process that force the consulting firms to collaborate rather than compete, so you can learn from all of them not just one • To compensate for the additional time being put in by the consulting firms, ensure that the remainder of the sales cycle is as short as possible and focuses on the specific needs of the project, rather than, for example, the generic attributes of the consulting firms	• Invest time working with your client in order to ensure the scope of the work is clear and realistic • Be willing to work with a subset of your competitors in order to share ideas and experience, if not your detailed data and methodology

Objective: To ensure that the contribution of each participant in the consulting ecosystem is recognised and rewarded		
Main barriers to achieving it	**Actions the client can take**	**Actions the consultants can take**
• Clients and suppliers assume that a bilateral relationship between the two main parties is the best way to organise a project • People talk about "working in partnership" without any clear idea of what this means in practice	• Put in place commercial arrangements between you, your IT suppliers and consulting firms which ensure an equitable structure, transparency and collective reward based on the achievement of your business objectives • Make it clear to all those involved in the ecosystem (from your side, as well as your suppliers') the type of behaviour and ways of working you expect	• Work with your client and other suppliers as equal partners, being clear about what each party contributes

Objective: To ensure that the senior executives sponsoring the project, and the consulting firm itself are publicly committed to success		
Main barriers to achieving it	**Actions the client can take**	**Actions the consultants can take**
• Senior managers are not consulted about the decision to bring consultants in and are therefore unwilling to make their time available • More junior staff take their lead from their bosses and do not take the project seriously	• Ensure that you involve all senior stakeholders at an early stage and keep them informed of progress • Develop a realistic plan for the project that makes clear what commitment is required from these people and liaise with them in advance to make sure that they are available and attend the meetings they have promised to come to	• Coach your client where necessary to liaise with senior people in other parts of their organisation • Ensure that meetings involving senior people are scheduled as early as possible, ideally during the preliminary planning stages and before the final timescales have been agreed so that you can factor in any likely delays at this stage

Objective: To put in place, from the outset of a project, the metrics that will help drive successful outcomes		
Main barriers to achieving it	**Actions the client can take**	**Actions the consultants can take**

• Organisations tend to develop business cases for projects that assume the involvement of consultants, rather than treating it as a discrete item to be evaluated separately
• The amorphous and varied nature of consulting makes it hard to quantify the value added
• Human nature means that people rarely welcome being scrutinised over any decisions
	• Ensure that you develop two separate business cases for a project, one that quantifies the costs and benefits if you rely solely on internal resources and one that looks how both costs and benefits change when you involve consultants
	• Focus on a small number of metrics that capture the impact your consultants will or have had:
	  • Taking better decisions
	  • Executing plans more effectively and efficiently
	  • Improving the capability of your staff and managers
	• Ask yourself what would have been different if you had not involved them
		• Prompt your clients to think about success metrics before the project starts, not at the end; this will also help you focus on what your client values most
		• Ensure that a proper review of the project takes place once it has been completed, with you and the client being honest about what could have been improved. Rather than making a client think the worse of you, you will find that it actually earns you more respect

Objective: To communicate effectively with those involved with the project, or affected by it, and irrespective of their level in the organisation		
Main barriers to achieving it	**Actions the client can take**	**Actions the consultants can take**

• Senior managers and project managers assume that they simply have to send out an email for people further down the organisational hierarchy to know what is going on	• Send out a clear and consistent message:
	  • Through all layers of your organisation, ensuring that even the most junior people understand what is going on and why consultants are needed to help
	  • Across your organisation as a whole (consulting projects often have an indirect impact on different areas of an organisation and it is just as important for these people to know what is happening)
		• Work with your client to communicate effectively
		• Ensure the messages you give out are consistent with those of your client
		• Let them know if you think their messages have not penetrated deep or wide enough in their organisation

Objctive: To ensure the consultants take a flexible approach to the project, accommodating new ideas where appropriate		
Main barriers to achieving it	**Actions the client can take**	**Actions the consultants can take**
• Clients look for magical solutions, either from the "thought leadership" consulting firms publish or from the consulting process itself • Consulting firms are not willing to adapt their approach to suit a client's unique set of circumstances	• Use thought leadership judiciously, focusing on whether it will help you achieve your ends, rather than expecting it to provide a checklist for guaranteed success • Expect genuine insights from your consultants, but not grandiose theories	• Remember that every client is different • Ensure that you listen to what your client has to say • Adapt your approach to suit them, rather than force them to fit in with your established way of working

Objective: To ensure that the skills and knowledge of the consultants are transferred to your own staff so they do not become dependent on the consultants		
Main barriers to achieving it	**Actions the client can take**	**Actions the consultants can take**
• Complex organisations do not invest sufficient time and effort into skills transfer but assume it will happen by osmosis • Consulting firms can be concerned that they will cannibalise the opportunity for future work	• Be clear about what type of knowledge (technical) "intimacy" and experience you want to acquire from your consultants • Put in place specific actions (secondments, coaching, etc) to ensure this will take place • Ensure there is enough time and money in the consulting project plan to enable this to happen	• Work with your client to ensure a definite programme in which specific skills are passed on to individuals • Recognise that effective skills transfer is more likely to win you clients in the future, than lose them

Objective: To create recognition and rewards that motivate internal staff to put in the extra effort required for success		
Main barriers to achieving it	**Actions the client can take**	**Actions the consultants can take**
• Cynicism: people don't expect the consultants to add value • People feel alienated and marginalised by the presence of consultants, and expect their careers to suffer as a result	• Staff the project with people who have (or can be given) a reason for wanting to make it succeed • Make this reason explicit, a "contract" between you and them that is dependent on the success of the overall project	• Speak to all the individual people who work on your project from your client's organisation in order to understand what they would like to get from the project at a personal level • Provide regular feedback to your client about their performance and coach them to improve where necessary • Work with your client to ensure that these people get the rewards and/or recognition they deserve

Objective: To establish integrated teams of client staff and consultants		
Main barriers to achieving it	**Actions the client can take**	**Actions the consultants can take**
• The presence of consultants is resented by internal staff • The consultants work in a separate office and have a demonstrably different culture	• Reduce discomfort in the project team by establishing a clear set of rules and clarifying who is responsible for what • Ensure everyone works in the same location, subject to the same set of "rules" • Invest time and money understanding individuals' strengths and weaknesses • Ensure that tough deadlines are met early in the project so you (and the project team) can see who does and who does not contribute • Replace people who are not contributing swiftly	• Ensure that the consultants you put on the project do not think they are "better" than your client's staff • Make sure your consultants stay on your client's site as much as possible • If the personal chemistry of a team is not working, be willing to move people around

And if your project is an international one...

Objective: To ensure that you have the appropriate structure before you start		
Main barriers to achieving it	**Actions the client can take**	**Actions the consultants can take**
• A failure to think through precisely what the project is intended to achieve and how the project team are expected to deal with the (inevitably) conflicting demands of different local operations	• Decide how you want the project to achieve its objectives, as this will determine the structure and approach you adopt: • Do you want to drive compliance to a single, international standard? • Do you want to understand the different needs of, say, different consumer or employee groups? • Choose a consulting firm that is culturally suited to this approach, one that emphasises a single, common culture across all its offices or one that allows local offices to develop their own culture and style • Create a project team that reflects your need for homogeneity or heterogeneity	• Ensure that you understand not just what your client wants to achieve but how • Choose the composition of your consulting team based on these requirements

Acknowledgements

"Be advised" has been made possible by the collective endeavor of our consulting community, who have shared with us their experiences and valuable client insight, gained from close and long term relationships. Together, we have been able to create this informative guide, based on expert advice formed through many years and a wide base of experience.

It is with pleasure therefore, that we present to you those consultants who have contributed to this book:

Vincent Berthelon, Managing Director for the Industry sector in France and at an international level, graduated from Ecole Centrale Paris. After more than 10 years experience in the management consulting field for companies such as Andersen Consulting and Transiciel Cisa, focusing on R&D improvement, supply chain and industrial maintenance, and large-scale ERP projects, he joined Logica Business Consulting in 2000. Most notably he has piloted transformation projects for Total, Arcelor, Renault and EDF DPN. Concurrently, Vincent has led the creation of the Logica Business Consulting network, organized in international practices, with 3,500 consultants in 6 European countries.

Patrik Wentjärvi is head of the Consulting practice in Logica Sweden where he manages vertical and horizontal Consulting Business Teams. His focus is on advising mainly large clients in areas such as organizational transformation and performance management; helping them achieve measurable bottom-line improvement and lasting change.

Rupert Baddeley leads the Strategic Change stream within the UK's Business Change Management team. He has worked across a number of sectors helping clients improve their revenues and margins through operational improvement, performance management and cost reduction. He also applies his skills in creative and innovative thinking to help clients address their strategic issues from new perspectives.

Paulo Magro da Luz is the Managing Director for the Public & Financial Sectors and is in charge of Business Consulting at Logica Iberia. He has a large experience in both sectors having worked previously in Accenture, Cap Gemini and Novabase, the Portuguese IT leader. He has also had direct experience in the Portuguese Public Administration Reform as Executive Coordinator for a previous government.

Phil Barnett leads the UK Local Government team providing senior engagement with clients to drive efficiency and effectiveness into their services. Phil also leads Logica's Local Government European focus group which looks to leverage best practice from across Europe to the betterment of services to citizens provided through Local Government in regions, municipalities and city areas.

Taneli Hallanaro is the leader of the Business Consulting sector in Finland. He has worked with many of the leading Nordic companies helping clients to focus and revitalize their business. Taneli has a solid background in Customer Relationship Management and Enterprise Architecture planning. Taneli is a member of Logica's Cloud Computing development team.

Benoit Leboucher joined Logica Business Consulting in 2005 and serves as the Sourcing International Business Team Leader. He has 20 years experience in consulting and his specialties include Information System, supply chain, and purchasing. Benoit earned his Engineering degree in Mathematics and MBA from Paris University.

Acknowledgements

Dr. Geleyn Meijer is a partner at Logica and strategy director of Logica Business Consulting Netherlands. He pioneered Logica's innovation policy and leads Logica's active participation in strategic business developments with clients and alliance partners across the EU. Geleyn is initiator and board member of the Services Innovation programme for the Creative and Financial sector. A programme launched with Logica's clients and partners to stimulate the take-up of ICT-led services industry.

He is associate professor at the University of Amsterdam and publishes on the development of 3rd generation management consultancies where technology, creativity and entrepreneurship are cornerstones.

Gonçalo Serra is the Business Consulting Director for Logica Iberia. He helps clients transform their organization, focusing on IT innovation and cost reduction. Before joining Logica, Gonçalo was IT & Innovation manager in an Oil & Gas company and responsible for the Portuguese Government Public Procurement Programme. He teaches in National Public Schools and universities. He is co-author of a book on IT Transformation.

Sébastien Durand is Associate Director at Logica Business Consulting. He joined the firm in 1999 where he founded the practice dedicated to the corporate function performance optimization and international business transformation. After graduating in Industrial Chemistry from the Universities of Lyon and Euro Mediterranean, Sébastien Durand began his career by creating the MDH consulting company in 1997, specialized in the optimization of the procurement function. He is the author of several publications including "The consultant in crisis" (1997), management books on governance optimization and contributed to the book "consulting internationally" (2010). He has managed several international transformation programs in different industries.

Oliver Mark is in charge of Sustainability at Logica Business Consulting in Germany. He leads the service portfolio and engages customers around Sustainability from strategy to implementation. As the Environmental Officer he is responsible for defining and implementing all activities in the areas of energy efficiency and environmental protection. He is OpenGroup Master Certified IT Architect and has published ten books and many articles.

We would like to take this opportunity to thank our consulting community as a whole, including the clients who shared with us their advice and words of wisdom for the benefit of all, to enable us to truly "be brilliant together".

Index

Be advised

Achevé d'imprimer sur rotative par l'Imprimerie Darantiere à Dijon-Quetigny
Dépôt légal :
N° d'impression : 10-0968

Imprimé en France